FORD
MUSTANG

Brad Bowling

motorbooks

Quarto is the authority on a wide range of topics.

Quarto educates, entertains and enriches the lives of our readers—enthusiasts and lovers of hands-on living.

www.quartoknows.com

First published in 2010 by Motorbooks, an imprint of Quarto Publishing Group USA Inc., 400 First Avenue North, Suite 400, Minneapolis, MN 55401 USA. Telephone: (612) 344-8100 Fax: (612) 344-8692

quartoknows.com
Visit our blogs at quartoknows.com

Motorbooks titles are also available at discounts in bulk quantity for industrial or sales-promotional use. For details write to Special Sales Manager at Quarto Publishing USA Inc., 400 First Avenue North, Suite 400, Minneapolis, MN 55401 USA.

To find out more about our books, visit us online at www.motorbooks.com.

Library of Congress Cataloging-in-Publication Data

Bowling, Brad.
 Ford Mustang / Brad Bowling.
    p. cm.
 Includes index.
 ISBN 978-0-7603-3808-7 (sb w/ flaps)
 1. Mustang automobile—History. 2. Mustang automobile—Pictorial works. I. Title.
  TL215.M8B66 2010
  629.222'2—dc22

2010023624

On the front cover: This is a replica of the 1968 *Bullitt* Mustang made famous by Steve McQueen. The Mustang underwent its first re-design in 1967, gaining two inches in length and 2.7 inches in width. Ford gave the 2+2 body a full fastback roofline that extended from the windshield header to the tip of the trunk lid. *Robert Kerian/Transtock*

On the back cover, top: For only $2,368, just about any hard-working American in 1964 could park a new Mustang in the driveway of his ranch-style home. That base-model pony would have a hardtop body with a 170-cubic-inch inline six-cylinder engine and three-speed manual transmission. **Middle:** In 1984, Ford Motor Co. tried once again to make the American driving enthusiast love turbochargers when it introduced its world-class SVO Mustang. **Bottom:** In 2006, Shelby sold a batch of identical black-and-gold 500 GT-350H fastbacks to Hertz (for its Fun Collection) with 4.6-liter SOHC V-8s putting 325 horsepower through five-speed automatic transmissions and 3.55:1 axle gears.

On the frontis: Through the clever use of fiberglass and some taillight lenses from the Ford parts bin, Shelby created a longer car that bore little resemblance to the standard Mustang. The addition of inboard headlights and multiple scoops made the Shelby resemble an exotic race car.

Editor: Peter Schletty
Design Manager: Kou Lor
Designed by: Heather Parlato
Cover designed by: John Sticha

Printed in China

CONTENTS

ABOUT THE PHOTOS AND CAR OWNERS

All photography in this book was performed by the author, unless otherwise indicated below. Here is a list of individual cars profiled in this publication, accompanied by recognition of the people who owned them at the time they were photographed.

1964½ convertible – Monty Seawright
1964½ Indy Pace Car – Drew Takach
1966 2+2 – Steve Markham
1966 Shelby GT-350H – Greg Sullins
1966 Shelby GT-350R (Photos Jerry Heasley)
1967 2+2 GTA – Dave Goff
1967 hardtop – Allison Goff
1967 T-5 convertible – Johnnie and
   Rachel Garner
1968 T-5 convertible – Johnnie and
   Rachel Garner
1968 California Special – Joel Franckowiak
1968 Shelby GT-500 – Monty Seawright
1969 Mach 1 428 – Craig Cox
1969 Grandé – Sam Dean
1970 Mach 1 – Mike Rayburn
1970 Shelby GT-500 convertible – Wert family
1969 Boss 302 – Monty Seawright
1970 Boss 429 – Aaron Scott
1971 hardtop – Chip Peyton
1971 Mach 1 429 CJ – Miles DeCoste
1971 Boss 351 – Alan Goodman
1972 Sprint convertible – Ben Mandell
1972 HO hardtop – Pat Szyslowski
1973 hardtop – Greg Sullins
1973 Mach 1 – Eric Helms
1974 Mustang II (Photos Jerry Heasley)
1976 Cobra II – Lou McCoy

1978 King Cobra – Monty Seawright
1979 Indy Pace Car Replica – Monty
   Seawright and Daniel Carpenter
1982 GT – Monty Seawright
1984 GT-350 – Monty Seawright
1984 Saleen – Stu Akers
1984–1986 SVO – Monty Seawright
1985 Twister II – Monty Seawright
1987 GT – Keith Jones
1989 Saleen SSC – Monty Seawright and
   Mark LaMaskin
1990-1993 Saleen SC – Bill Price
1992 Special Service Vehicle –
   Michael Morrison
1992 Steeda – Sergio Perciballi
1993 Cobra and Cobra R – Jimmy Morrison
1994 GT – Mike Kelly
1994 SVT Cobra Indy Pace Car –
   Dennis Reardon
1994 Saleen S-351 – Terry Denton
1994 Saleen SR – Mark LaMaskin
1995 SVT Cobra R – Michael Morrison
1996 SVT Cobra Mystic – Monty Seawright
1996 Saleen S-281 Cobra – Lee Davis
1998 V-6 – Jimmy Morrison
1998 GT – Jimmy Morrison
1999 GT – Jimmy Morrison
1999 SVT Cobra – Mark LaMaskin

1999 Saleen S-351 – Jimmy Morrison
2001 Bullitt – Steve Fowler
2001 Roush Stage III – Carol Barker
2003 SVT Cobra 10th Anniversary –
    Michael Morrison
2003 Roush Boyd Coddington California
    Roadster – Jimmy Morrison
2003 Mach 1 – Ford Motor Co. (Photos Ford)
2005 V-6 and GT – Ford Motor Co.
    (Photos Ford)

2006 Shelby GT-H – Greg Sullins
2007 Shelby GT-H – Greg Sullins
2007 Shelby GT – Greg Sullins
2007 Saleen/Parnelli Jones – Greg Sullins
2008 Bullitt – Al Rogers (Photos Al Rogers)
2008 SMS 25th Anniversary – Steve Saleen
2008 Shelby GT-500KR – Shelby
2010 GT – Ford Motor Co. (Photos Ford)
2010 Shelby GT-500 – Shelby (Photos Shelby)
2010 Roush 427 – Roush (Photos Roush)

INTRODUCTION

Four major factors led to the creation of Ford Motor Company's phenomenally successful Mustang in 1964: having the right guy in charge of product planning, the influence of sporty foreign cars, the repeal of an industry-wide racing ban, and sophisticated research into buyer demographics.

Lee Iacocca joined Ford Motor Company in 1946 as an industrial engineer but soon found his outgoing personality was better suited for the sales department. His creativity with such programs as the "56 for '56" campaign (which featured $56 monthly payments for 1956 Fords) earned him the position of vice president of the company's car-and-truck group by 1960.

During his early years in the business, Iacocca had observed post–World War II soldiers coming home with an appreciation for small, athletic MGs, Fiats, and Jaguars they had seen and driven in Europe. He also saw firsthand how the public fell in love with Ford's 1955 to 1957 two-seat Thunderbird, which was the American interpretation of a low, good-handling roadster.

In 1957, to prevent Congress from imposing safety restrictions on the industry, Ford, GM, and Chrysler (under the umbrella of the Automobile Manufacturers' Association) agreed to suspend factory support of motorsports and de-emphasize speed in their marketing and development of new models. Although Ford stuck to the spirit and letter of the law, Chevrolet and Pontiac flouted the ban and quickly dominated the major forms of racing through the backdoor support of their engineering departments.

Suffering defeat in the high-profile motorsports community made Ford products unexciting, and that was bad news for sales to young people. Research showed that the first wave of the postwar population boom was hitting the beach, so to speak. Millions of voting, educated, affluent Americans would want sporty, sexy cars by 1965, yet, in 1960, Ford was still promoting its stodgy models as safe and reliable. The compact Falcon was Ford's only car aimed at the youth market, and it was a rather plain-looking economy car. General Motors had its rear-engine Chevy Corvair—an innovative but unusually styled car that sold well, although traditional buyers were leery of its advanced engineering. Chrysler's volume model was the sturdy-but-dull Dodge Dart.

Iacocca recognized that the American auto industry had a serious "youth problem" on its hands and that the first person to serve that young audience would win all the marbles.

After being put in charge of the passenger-car division in 1960, Iacocca quickly called together Ford's most creative thinkers and members of the J. Walter Thompson advertising agency. This group, which came to be known as the Fairlane Committee (because it met at Dearborn's new Fairlane Hotel), met weekly for three-and-a-half months to discuss a strategy that would bring life back to the blue oval and win over a new generation of enthusiastic drivers. They addressed every aspect of Ford's production and competition models, outlining a program that would shortly be known as the Total Performance campaign. The cornerstone of Total Performance was the creation of a new four-passenger car with the appeal of the first-generation Thunderbird, European-influenced styling, and a range of high-performance V-8 models. It would debut in 1964, weigh less than 2,500 pounds, and cost less than $2,500 (due to its reliance on major Falcon parts already in production). A year and a half after the first Fairlane Committee meeting, Henry Ford II announced his company would no longer abide by the AMA ban, effectively pulling the trigger on Iacocca's Total Performance program.

Many, many drawings and full-scale models were submitted and rejected for the "special Falcon" project. Consideration was even given to some off-the-wall suggestions, such as the XT-Bird, which was literally a revival of the 1955 to 1957 Thunderbird with updated fenders and a tiny rear seat. The first real "aha" moment came in mid-1961 when Iacocca saw a model built by Ford Advanced Styling called the Allegro. Although it does not resemble what we now know to be the Mustang, Allegro featured a long hood, upright passenger compartment, and short trunk—the profile that would eventually carry through 45-plus years of Mustang design.

A year after seeing the Allegro, Iacocca asked three studios (Corporate Projects Advanced, Ford, and Lincoln-Mercury) to compete for the final exterior body look. Dave Ash and Joe Oros, from the Ford studio, turned in the winning design, which was known as the Cougar. Photos of this full-scale mockup reveal that the Cougar became the Mustang with very few changes.

And that's the story of how a nice Italian boy from Allentown, Pennsylvania, became the father of the Mustang phenomenon.

CHAPTER 1

FIRST GENERATION:
MUSTANG SETS THE PACE

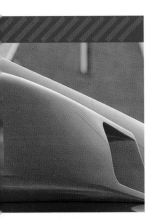

The Mustang's debut on April 17, 1964, grabbed the world's attention with an intensity seldom generated by mere automobiles. Only the interest surrounding Ford's Model A—that much-anticipated follow-up to Henry's long-lived Model T—could compare, and that had been 45 years earlier!

The Mustang did not appear at the start of the 1964 model year, but six months in, as an "early" 1965 (although modern collectors inaccurately refer to these as 1964 1/2 models). Half-year new-car introductions were still rare in the 1960s, but Lee Iacocca promoted the idea as a way to have his Mustang stand out from the herd. Such a scheme had already worked well with the Falcon Futura and Galaxie 500XL Sports Hardtop.

While Ford's various departments had been slow to embrace the Mustang early in its development—they had been burned very recently by the disastrous 1958 to 1960 Edsel—by the time production started, the whole company believed in it.

Convincing car buyers of the Mustang's uniqueness required nothing more than showing some photos. The buzz was so deafening that Iacocca and the Mustang appeared on the covers of *Time* and *Newsweek* simultaneously.

Ford's advertising blitz leading up to the release included ads in 2,600 newspapers (reaching 75 percent of the country), 24 magazines (covering 68 million readers), and an unprecedented three-network buy from 9:30 to 10 p.m. on April 16 (viewed by more than half of the households in America). In an age when the internet, iPods, and cell phones can instantly provide any information you request, it is difficult to realize that many people watched TV that night in 1964 just to see those highly publicized Mustang commercials.

What customers saw when they flooded their local Ford dealers were a hardtop and convertible that came standard with equipment that would cost extra on more-mundane vehicles. Bucket seats, a floor-mounted shifter, carpeting, and full gauges are commonplace today, but buyers in the 1960s felt like they were driving home in something truly exotic. More than 22,000 Mustangs were ordered on that first day, and Ford was pumping them out at full speed in Dearborn, Michigan; Metuchen, New Jersey; and San Jose, California.

The excitement continued as Ford rolled out more engine, body, and model options. Just before the end of its first half year on the market, the Mustang was available with a 271-horsepower 289-cubic-inch V-8. The Mustang also received a beautiful fastback body option known as the 2+2. As if those two additions weren't enough to put the Mustang at the top of the performance class, Le Mans racer and Cobra creator Carroll Shelby introduced his track-ready version of the pony car called the GT-350 just before the official start of 1965 production.

What we now consider to be the Mustang's first generation actually encompasses four visually different models. Ford slightly enlarged

the car overall for 1967, presumably to better handle available big-block V-8s. Following industry trends, there was another growth spurt for 1969 and yet another in 1971 that would last until the line was re-imagined as the smaller, less-powerful Mustang II.

The 1967 to 1968 years only improved the Mustang's performance image, raising the bar for its competitors with a four-barrel 390-cubic-inch V-8 that produced 320 horsepower. In the middle of the 1968 model year, Ford stuffed a 428-cubic-inch, 335-horsepower V-8 between the fenders and created one of the fastest street cars available.

The Total Performance campaign peaked in 1969, when Ford offered a total of eight V-8 engines to Mustang buyers and created the wildly popular Mach 1 SportsRoof package. Ford also gave birth to a set of Mustang twins that year known as the Boss 302 and 429, which were the closest anyone could get to driving a race car on the street.

By 1971, the public's fascination with power and speed was fading, and the extra-large ponies (more like Clydesdales at this point) reflected that lack of enthusiasm. In the final year of the first generation, there were but four engine choices—only three of which were V-8s, and only one of which was fitted with a four-barrel carburetor.

For only $2,368, just about any hard-working American in 1964 could park a new Mustang in the driveway of his ranch-style home. That base-model pony would have a hardtop body with a 170-cubic-inch, inline six-cylinder engine and a three-speed manual transmission. Standard creature comforts included vinyl-padded interior surfaces, bucket seats, a floor-mounted shifter, carpet, and a mat on the trunk floor.

Very few people bought *that* car, however, because the Mustang's marketing campaign

1964½ - 1966

Price: $2,368 (six-cylinder hardtop)
Engine: 170-cid, six-cylinder, 101 horsepower
260-cid, V-8, 164 horsepower
289-cid, V-8, 210 horsepower
289-cid, V-8, 271 horsepower
0–60 mph: 7.5 seconds (289/271 V-8, four-speed, 4.11:1 axle)
Top Speed: 117 mph

encouraged a look at the long list of optional equipment that could be applied to the hardtop, convertible, or (later in the year) 2+2 body styles. By the end of the 1964 sales season, 120,000 Mustangs had been built, only 27 percent carrying the base six-cylinder engine. Most were equipped with the 260- and 289-cubic-inch V-8s Ford offered, and there was even a 271-horsepower 289 in late 1964. Half of the cars were fitted with automatic transmissions, and another 20 percent upgraded to the four-speed manuals.

As expected, 99 percent of those Mustangs were equipped with the heater (which could be deleted for credit), and only 6.4 percent paid extra for air conditioning.

After less than two years of production, the Mustang chalked up 1,000,000 sales, a phenomenal milestone Ford celebrated with a series of ads that asked, "What do you do after you build a million Mustangs?" The answer followed: "Start on the second million!"

Did You Know?

On May 30, 1964, the new Mustang performed pace car duties during the 48th Indianapolis 500. Three convertibles were modified with 271-horsepower V-8s, and 35 stock convertibles served VIPs during the event. Afterward, Ford produced fewer than 200 pace car replicas as part of a celebratory competition among dealers. Very few have been located.

Le Mans winner and father of the Cobra roadsters Carroll Shelby produced his own high-performance version of Ford's Mustang from 1965 to 1970. The first-year GT-350 came only as a Wimbledon White fastback with a 306-horsepower, 289-cubic-inch V-8; four-speed manual transmission; and a long list of chassis upgrades. They were thinly disguised race cars for the street; the stiff suspensions, fiberglass hoods, loud exhausts, trunk-mounted batteries, stripper interiors, Goodyear

1965 - 1966 SHELBY

Price: $4,547
Engine: 289-cid, V-8, 306 horsepower
0–60 mph: 5.7 seconds
Top Speed: 133 mph

Photo by Jerry Heasley

Blue Dot high-performance street rubber, and popular Guardsman Blue competition stripes distinguished them from standard Mustangs. The '65 GT-350 had no rear seat—instead, a fiberglass panel acted as a cargo area floor to trim weight and allow the car to compete in Sports Car Club of America–sanctioned races as a two-seater. Amazingly, Shelby Mustangs were covered by Ford's warranty.

For 1966, Shelby's Mustang softened a little, offering automatic transmissions, a variety of colors, back seats, friendlier suspension setups, and AM radios. Ford Motor Company influenced this decision because dealers had a hard time justifying the GT-350's high price and rough ride. Base price for the decontented fastback dropped from $4,547 to $4,428. The strategy worked because GT-350 sales rose from 562 cars in 1965 to 2,378 in 1966.

Did You Know?

In 1965, Shelby produced 36 race-built GT-350s known today as the R-models that sold for $5,995 each. Their 289-cubic-inch engines were rated between 325 and 350 horsepower. A year later, Shelby sold 1,001 GT-350s to the Hertz rental car agency to be used in its Sports Car Club program.

The Mustang underwent its first re-design in 1967, gaining two inches in length and 2.7 inches in width. Ford gave the 2+2 body a full fastback roofline that extended from the windshield header to the tip of the trunk lid. Overall, the Mustang looked like the successful sporty car everyone fell in love with in 1964—just slightly bigger. Ford was wise not to mess with this formula because competitors Chevrolet and Pontiac

1967 - 1968

Price: $2,461 (six-cylinder hardtop)

Engine: 200-cid, six-cylinder, 120 horsepower

289-cid, V-8, 200 horsepower

289-cid, V-8, 225 horsepower

289-cid, V-8, 271 horsepower

390-cid, V-8, 320 horsepower

0–60 mph: 7.3 seconds (390/320 V-8, automatic, 3.00:1 axle)

Top Speed: 124 mph

entered the pony car market in full force in 1967 with their Camaro and Firebird. (Even Ford's sister division Mercury introduced its Cougar with that model year.)

The larger body gave the Mustang more room to carry bigger powerplants. For 1967, that meant a big-block 390-cubic-inch, 320-horsepower V-8 option; a year later, Ford gave hot shoes a chance to move up to the 428-cubic-inch, 335-horsepower Cobra Jet. Model year 1968 also brought with it several pieces of federally mandated equipment, including side marker reflectors, a padded steering wheel, a seatbelt system with shoulder harnesses (hardtops and fastbacks only), and adjustable headrests on the bucket seats.

A two-month strike by Ford workers limited the Mustang's production for 1968.

Did You Know?

Ford offered a special GTA cosmetic and performance package in 1967 that could only be ordered with one of the four V-8 engines and an automatic transmission. The package included four-inch driving lamps, power front disc brakes, low-restriction exhausts with quad outlets, rocker-panel stripes, and special handling equipment, such as higher-rate springs and shock absorbers.

Ford dealers had once complained that the premium-priced Shelby Mustangs looked too much like their Ford cousins and had too many expensive high-performance parts to maintain. Those dealers were ecstatic over the 1967 and 1968 line, which bore little cosmetic resemblance to the Mustang, but was nearly identical mechanically. Through the clever use of fiberglass and some taillight lenses from the Ford parts bin, Shelby created a longer car that bore little resemblance to the standard Mustang. The addition of inboard headlights and multiple scoops made the Shelby resemble an exotic race car. The competition theme showed itself inside the car in the form of a two-point roll bar that mounted shoulder harnesses and inertia reels.

One-upping Ford's introduction of the 390-cubic-inch big-block V-8, Shelby added the 428 Police Interceptor–powered GT-500

to the lineup at the start of 1967. Both cars were available as fastbacks only in '67, but a convertible crept into the family for 1968, as did a GT-500KR powered by a 428-cubic-inch Cobra Jet V-8.

In spite of the flashier bodies, Shelby Mustang prices dropped for the second year in a row, reaching $3,995 (GT-350) and $4,195 (GT-500) in 1967. Prices increased in 1968 to $4,116 and $4,317, respectively.

1967 - 1968 SHELBY

Price: $3,995 (GT-350)
$4,195 (GT-500)
Engine: 289-cid, V-8, 306 horsepower
428-cid, V-8, 355 horsepower
0–60 mph: 5.4 seconds (428/355, four-speed, 3.25:1 axle)
Top Speed: 129 mph

Did You Know?

Shelby GT-350 and GT-500 production relocated at the start of the 1968 model year from Los Angeles to Ionia, Michigan. Shelby's lease at the airport facility ran out, and it made sense for the cars to be built closer to their source of Canadian fiberglass panels.

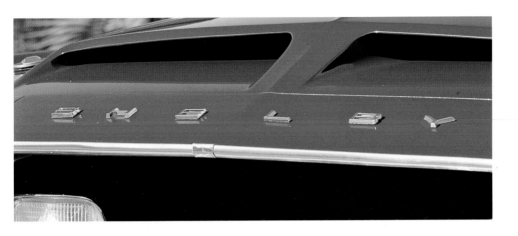

Responsible for 20 percent of all Mustang and Thunderbird sales in America, the West Coast Ford dealers were an influential group in the 1960s. In 1968, they were responsible for creating and promoting a very unusual cosmetic package for the Mustang that has a tremendous following today. It was called the GT/CS California Special, and it could only be purchased in hardtop form. The Shelby-influenced design featured a pair of rectangular driving lights, GT-350-style deck lid with built-in spoiler, that year's sequential taillights, and a blacked-out grille empty of Mustang identification.

1968 CALIFORNIA SPECIAL

Price: $2,602 (base) plus cost of package
Engine: 200-cid, inline six-cylinder, 115 horsepower
289-cid, V-8, 195 horsepower
302-cid, V-8, 220 horsepower
302-cid, V-8, 230 horsepower
390-cid, V-8, 280 horsepower
390-cid, V-8, 325 horsepower
428-cid, V-8, 335 horsepower
0-60 mph: 9.7 seconds (289/225, four-speed, 3.00:1 axle)
Top Speed: 110 mph

Because it was purely an appearance upgrade, the GT/CS look could be ordered with any engine/transmission combination, so there were six-cylinder California Specials as well as 428-cubic-inch V-8 versions. Dealers announced 5,000 of these special ponies would be produced, but the final tally came to 4,118.

Denver-area Ford dealerships, which had been selling their own regional Mustang customs since the 1966 model year (with only special paint and emblems to distinguish them), ordered a small number of the GT/CS cars wearing High Country

Special badges. All GT/CS and High Country Special cars were built in the San Jose, California, Ford plant.

Did You Know?

The California Special's look was inspired by a Shelby prototype known as Little Red. This hardtop, fitted with a supercharged 428-cubic-inch V-8, '67 GT-350/500 taillights, and black vinyl top, got plenty of attention at new car shows but never went into production. Shelby Automotive engineered the GT/CS components.

The 1969 to 1970 Mustangs could be ordered with a dizzying array of engines, transmissions, body styles, options, and models. Horsepower war had been declared against Chevrolet, Oldsmobile, Dodge, and Plymouth, and Ford intended to win every battle!

In 1969, Ford introduced the Mach 1, Boss 302, and Boss 429—performance machines based on its new SportsRoof fastback design. Shelby, of course, had its convertible and fastback GT-350 and GT-500 in the fight.

1969 - 1970

Price: $2,618
Engine: 200-cid, inline six-cylinder, 115 horsepower
250-cid, inline six-cylinder, 155 horsepower
302-cid, V-8, 220 horsepower
302-cid, V-8, 290 horsepower (Boss)
351-cid, V-8, 250 horsepower
351-cid, V-8, 290 horsepower
390-cid, V-8, 320 horsepower
428-cid, V-8, 335 horsepower (Cobra Jet)
428-cid, V-8, 360 horsepower (Super Cobra Jet)
429-cid, V-8, 370 horsepower (Boss)
0–60 mph: 5.5 seconds (428/335, automatic, 3.50:1 axle)
Top Speed: 121 mph

There were no less than eight V-8 engines available, from the base 302 with two-barrel carb, to the ground-pounding 429 that came only in the Boss 429. Ford also introduced a pair of 351-cubic-inch engines that year.

This proliferation of powerplants caused the Mustang to grow and gain some weight. It stretched 3.8 inches in overall length, while retaining the original car's 108-inch wheelbase. For 1969 only, the Mustang wore four round headlights, with the outer lenses deeply recessed into the fender openings and the inboard units set into the far ends of the grille.

Ford promoted the hardtop Mustang with a new Grandé model. This dress-up package included a vinyl roof, plush interior, deluxe two-spoke steering wheel, color-keyed mirrors, full wheel covers, electric clock, paint stripes, and luxury bucket seats—all for $231.

Did You Know?

The GT Equipment Group, the sportiest Mustang package from 1964 to 1968, was overshadowed by the new Mach 1. There were very few takers for the GT in its final year of 1969—only 4,973 coupes, convertibles, and fastbacks—but for $147, buyers got special handling equipment, racing stripes, dual exhausts, pin-type hood lock latches, and a simulated hood scoop.

The third and final version of Carroll Shelby's GT-350 and GT-500 bore little resemblance to the Mustang on which it was based—on the surface, that is. Fiberglass fenders, hood, and rear caps increased the GT-350/500's overall length by three inches. The hood was home to five recessed, triangular scoops. Rectangular driving lights sat below the bumper. Design themes from 1968 were repeated on the rear, including the fiberglass deck lid, integral spoiler, and sequential taillights.

1969 - 1970 SHELBY

Price: $4,434 (GT-350 fastback)
$4,709 (GT-500 fastback)
Engine: 351-cid, V-8, 290 horsepower
428-cid, V-8, 335 horsepower
0–60 mph: 6.0 seconds (428/335)
Top Speed: 115 mph

Under that scooped hood sat a largely unmodified 351 V-8 (in the GT-350) or 428 Cobra Jet (GT-500). Suspension and brakes were from the Ford heavy-duty bin, and

the GT-500 came standard with staggered shocks. The supply of Shelby-specific wheels was interrupted when a defect was discovered; Mustang Boss 302 rims were installed while the recall took place.

Shelby sales were down, reflecting the overcrowded muscle car market that included quite a few Ford Mustang models, such as the Mach 1 and Bosses. Rather than compete against Ford, Shelby made 1969 his final year of production. To sell late 1969 models, Shelby agreed to update them into 1970 specs with a set of black hood stripes, chin spoiler, and emissions control unit. The FBI oversaw the Shelby factory's conversion, but records do not indicate how many were modified.

Did You Know?

Where did the late '68 GT-500KR go? When Ford introduced its 428 Cobra Jet V-8 on April 1, 1968, Shelby replaced the GT-500's 428 Police Interceptor with that more-powerful V-8. He attached the "KR" initials to the newer version. The '69 GT-500 retained the Cobra Jet V-8 but lost the KR name.

Ford unleashed its Boss 302 and Boss 429 models on the public in 1969 for a very good reason—to homologate their very special engines for racing.

The high-revving, high-output 302-cubic-inch V-8 was built to compete against Chevy's Camaro on the Sports Car Club of America's Trans-American circuit. Its claimed 290 horsepower rating was an understatement chosen because the comparable Camaro listed the same output. The Boss 302 suspension was ready for the track, with high-rate springs, heavy-duty

1969 - 1970 BOSS

Price: $3,354 (Boss 302)
$3,826 (Boss 429)
Engine: 302-cid, V-8, 290 horsepower
429-cid, V-8, 375 horsepower
0–60 mph: 6.9 seconds (302/290, four-speed, 3.91:1 axle)
7.2 seconds (429/375, four-speed, 3.91:1 axle)
Top Speed: 118 mph (both models)

shocks (staggered in the rear), and a rear stabilizer bar. Standard front disc brakes were power assisted. To set it apart from lesser—presumably, "worker"—Mustangs,

the Boss 302 received a blackout treatment on the hood, deck lid, and lower back panel; dual exhausts; a black Boss tape scheme; and color-keyed dual racing mirrors.

The Boss 429 was Ford's way to get its most powerful engine ever into NASCAR. Ford felt it would be easier to sell the required copies of the 429 engine to the public if it were packaged in a Mustang instead of the Torino that would eventually carry it in competition. Because installation of the 429 required a lot of specialized manual labor, Ford contracted Kar Kraft, of Brighton, Michigan, to create its big-block Boss.

Did You Know?

During their two years of production, the Boss 302 and 429 sold far more than the number of units required by SCCA and NASCAR. SCCA specified 1,000 units; Ford built 8,642 1969 to 1970 Boss 302s. NASCAR required 500 cars; Kar Kraft produced 1,358 Boss 1969 to 1970 429s.

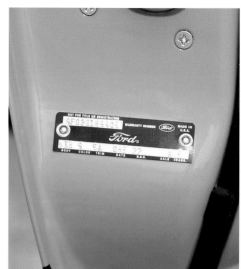

The Mustang rode on a 109-inch wheelbase (a 1-inch increase) for 1971, and everything else about the pony was bigger. Compared to the 1970 body, there was an extra 2.1 inches of overall length (to 189.5) and another 500 pounds of curb weight. Ford grew its Mustang big that year, anticipating the same demand for big-block power that had fueled sales for the previous four years. Unfortunately, the big car arrived just as the horsepower wars were winding down, leaving the once-svelte Mustang looking a little bloated.

1971

Price: $2,911

Engine: 250-cid, inline six-cylinder, 145 horsepower
302-cid, V-8, 210 horsepower
351-cid, V-8, 240 horsepower
351-cid, V-8, 285 horsepower (through May 1971)
351-cid, V-8, 280 horsepower (Cobra Jet)
351-cid, V-8, 330 horsepower (Boss)
429-cid, V-8, 370 horsepower (Cobra Jet)
429-cid, V-8, 375 horsepower (Super Cobra Jet)

0–60 mph: 6.5 seconds (429/370, automatic, 3.25:1 axle)
10 seconds (302/210, automatic, 2.79:1 axle)

Top Speed: 115 mph (429)
86 mph (302)

All three body styles—hardtop, fastback, and convertible—returned, as did the ever-popular Mach 1 and Grandé packages. Ford pared down the Mustang's engine options, offering seven V-8s, although not simultaneously. The 302 returned as base V-8, followed by four 351s that ranged in horsepower from 240 to 330. The real stars of the lineup—the 429-cubic-inch Cobra Jet and Super Cobra Jet—saw limited production of 1,250 units before being phased out. The two 429s were not related to the Boss 429 of 1969 and 1970; instead, they were destroked Thunderbird/Lincoln 460s topped with wedge heads. Regardless of heritage, the '71 429 represented the final year a big-block Mustang was available . . . ever!

Did You Know?

Power windows made their way onto the Mustang options list for the first time in 1971. Only 1.9 percent of that year's cars were built with this luxurious piece of equipment. Other rare options for 1971 included the adjustable steering column (3.3 percent), cruise control (0.3 percent), limited-slip differential (5.9 percent), and four-speed transmission (5.3 percent).

Ford's Boss Mustang program continued in 1971, this time built around its 351-cubic-inch, 330-horsepower V-8. The namesake engine featured solid lifters, four-bolt mains, large-port cylinder heads and valves, 11.7:1 compression, and aluminum valve covers. In other words, it was built to perform!

Like the Mach 1, the Boss 351 was available only in the fastback (or SportsRoof) body, and the two models bore a close resemblance. The Boss had a

1971 BOSS 351
Price: $4,124
Engine: 351-cid, V-8, 330 horsepower (Boss)
0–60 mph: 6.6 seconds
Top Speed: 100 mph

functional NASA-style hood with black or silver paint treatment, hood lock pins, and Ram Air engine decals. Additional Boss equipment included racing mirrors;

a honeycombed grille; hubcaps with trim rings; black or silver tape stripes; dual exhausts; power front disc brakes; a competition suspension with staggered rear shocks; a 3.91:1 Traction-Lok differential; a functional black spoiler, shipped "knocked-down" inside the car for dealer installation; an electronic RPM limiter; high-back bucket seats; a wide-ratio, four-speed manual transmission; a Hurst shifter; and blackwall tires. Ford installed a chrome bumper on the Boss, but the Mach 1–style color-keyed piece was an option.

Unlike the 1969 to 1970 Bosses, the 351 engine was not being homologated for any motorsports purpose. In spite of respectable sales for a $4,124 Mustang of 1,806 units, Ford dropped the Boss 351 in the middle of the year.

Did You Know?

Sports Car Graphic magazine tested the Boss 351 against Ford's own 429-powered Mustang in 1971 and found the big-block car to be only slightly faster. The 429 was only 0.3 seconds quicker to 60 miles per hour and 0.1 second quicker in the quarter-mile.

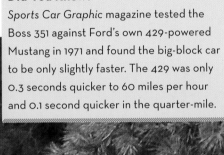

The big Mustang news for 1972 was a big drop in horsepower—at least, on paper. It's true the American auto industry was detuning its powerplants in the face of increased emissions requirements, but it was really the switch to SAE net horsepower standards that make 1972 look so dismal when compared to the previous year.

American cars had traditionally been advertised with their gross, or maximized, output, meaning the measurement did not take

1972

Price: $2,729
Engine: 250-cid, inline six-cylinder, 98 horsepower
302-cid, V-8, 140 horsepower
351-cid, V-8, 168 horsepower
351-cid, V-8, 200 horsepower (CJ)
351-cid, V-8, 275 horsepower (HO)
0–60 mph: 6.6 seconds (351/275, four-speed, 3.91:1 axle)
Top Speed: 120 mph

into account the real-world horsepower loss of accessories, a production exhaust system, and other factors. Under the new system, engines were tested and rated more realistically, and the Mustang's base engine (a 250-cubic-inch six-cylinder) dropped below 100 horsepower for the first time ever.

On the positive side, Mustang buyers could still order a peppy pony with a 351-cubic-inch, 275-horsepower High Output V-8. In a time of declining interest in performance cars, relatively few H.O. Mustangs were built, making this last-of-an-era model of exceptional interest to collectors.

The red-white-and-blue Sprint package brought patriotic fervor to the Mustang line in 1972. Ford dealers were limited to fastbacks and hardtops when ordering the Sprint, but 50 convertibles were built for use in the Washington, D.C., Cherry Day parade.

Did You Know?

Although its red-white-and-blue colors make the '72 Sprint a memorable model, it was not the first time Ford offered a Mustang Sprint. To move its slow-selling six-cylinder models in 1966, Ford promoted a Sprint 200 décor package that included a chrome air cleaner, center console, body side accent pinstripes, and wire wheel hubcaps.

Nineteen seventy-three marked the first time in Mustang history that Ford skipped the two-year model cycle and carried a design a third year. There were changes, however—none of them particularly desirable, such as the four-inch gain in overall length (to 194 inches) and extra weight that came with a mandatory front bumper upgrade. The engine lineup also continued to decline in power output, leaving performance

1973

Price: $2,729
Engine: 250-cid, inline six-cylinder, 98 horsepower
302-cid, V-8, 140 horsepower
351-cid, V-8, 177 horsepower
351-cid, V-8, 248 horsepower (CJ)
0–60 mph: 8.9 seconds (351/248, automatic, 3.25:1 axle)
Top Speed: 118 mph

enthusiasts with a 248-horsepower 351 four-barrel V-8 as their top choice. That sounds like a lot of grunt, until you remember it was paired to the heaviest Mustang body ever. Zero to 60 miles per hour with that 351 Cobra Jet was a leisurely nine-second trip. (Strangely, the 177-horsepower 351 with two-barrel carburetion could be ordered with Ram Air induction, but the four-barrel version could not.)

In the early 1970s, American car makers started eliminating convertible bodies from their product lines due to low customer interest. Ford, which offered the Mustang as its only 1973 ragtop option, announced there would be no convertible in the all-new 1974 lineup. This news doubled '73 convertible sales to more than 11,000 units and may have been responsible for a jump in the Mustang's overall popularity that year.

Did You Know?

Although Ford was about to introduce a Mustang designed from scratch in 1974, the big '73 received a sporty new wheel made of lightweight forged aluminum. The 14-inch rim cost an additional $111 on the Mach 1 and $119 on the Grandé hardtop and could be fitted with steel-belted radials.

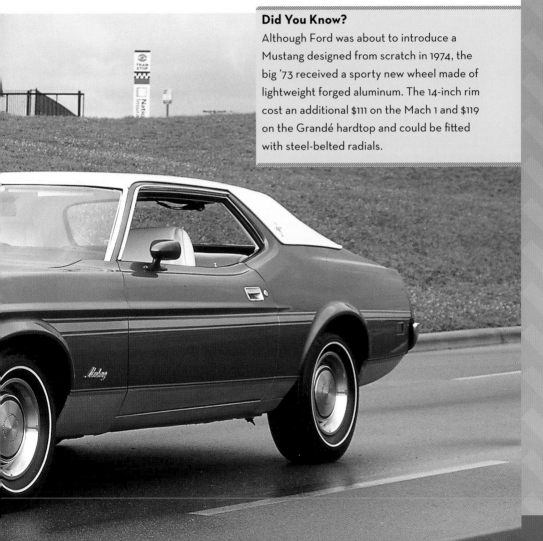

CHAPTER 2
SECOND GENERATION:
MUSTANG II—NO RESPECT

When Ford Motor Company introduced the 1974 Mustang II on August 28, 1973, everyone knew to expect a smaller car engineered to compete with sporty European and Japanese imports. The muscle car phenomenon that produced the Boss 429 and Super Cobra Jet was long dead.

Many factors influenced the Mustang II's engineers as they stared at their blank sheets of paper, including increased government-imposed emissions standards and rising insurance premiums for performance cars with young, often irresponsible, drivers. Ford also felt a public backlash for having turned the small, sporty 1955 Thunderbird into an overweight sedan and then repeating the pattern with the Mustang, which culminated in the giant 1971 to 1973 design. They were told the '74 car had to offer high value for its price, be sensibly sized, display a high level of engineering excellence, and be stylish.

Market planners replaced the Mustang's old powertrains with all-new hardware. Engine choices for 1974 were limited to a single-overhead-camshaft, 88-horsepower, 2.3-liter Lima four-cylinder (named for the Ohio factory that produced it) and Ford's German-built, 105-horsepower, 2.8-liter V-6. There was no V-8 available for 1974, but Ford listened to feedback from its customers and made structural changes to the engine compartment that allowed the company to offer one for 1975 to 1978—a 122-horsepower 302 (5.0-liter) with two-barrel carburetor. The decision required a longer hood, a repositioned radiator, new grille mounts, and a redesigned second crossmember.

To meet packaging goals, the new Mustang's 96.2-inch wheelbase was 11.8 inches shorter than the original. At 175 inches overall, it shrank quite a bit compared to the '65 (181.6) and '73 (189.5).

Providing a luxuriously smooth and quiet ride caused Ford to throw one innovation after another into the new pony—melting rubber sheets into the floorpan during assembly; a U-shaped, isolated subframe (aka, the "toilet seat"); and a larger-diameter driveshaft, to name a few.

Consumer clinics assembled a wish list of standard equipment for the Mustang IIs, all of which were fitted with tachometers, front disc brakes, sporty bucket seats, floor shifters, and simulated wood appliqués in the passenger compartment. A mere 16 months before Job One, data from those clinics also forced Ford to release the II in notchback *and* hatchback form; the company never entertained the idea of a Mustang II convertible, although it teased the show-car circuit with a targa-topped Sportiva.

Although many drawings and prototypes were reviewed during the 1974 model's design phase,

Ford ultimately chose the concept that most recalled the popular 1965 car. This look retained the original long-hood, short-deck theme. The wide grille, twin-headlamp treatment, sculpted side panels, and three-element taillight lenses said Mustang louder than the car's running-horse emblems.

To keep development costs as low as possible, Ford incorporated some components from the cheaper Pinto, which had been in production since the 1971 model year. On introduction, there were four Mustang II models to choose from: a base notchback (known simply as the Hardtop),

a base hatchback (2+2), an upscale notchback (Ghia), and a sporty hatchback (Mach 1).

Prices across the four-model lineup ranged from $3,081 to $3,621, but most dealers anticipated a repeat of the 1964 stampede, so showrooms were full of heavily optioned cars that stickered around $4,500. Even without the options, 1974 prices were up when compared model to model. For example, at $3,621, a new Mach 1 with V-6 cost $533 more than the previous year's Mach 1 with V-8.

The Mustang II received accolades from the press, such as when *Motor Trend* named it the Car of the Year, and advertising stressed the "Little

Jewel" aspect of the car, but high sticker prices and lack of a true performance model got sales off to a slower start than Ford wanted. On October 17, 1973, however, small, four-cylinder cars became very popular when the Organization of Petroleum Exporting Countries (OPEC) declared an oil embargo for political reasons, more than tripling the price of gasoline in some parts of the United States, when available at all. The Mustang II (which would become available with a gas-sipping MPG model in mid-June 1975) and Pinto stablemate were suddenly the right cars at the right time—a sentiment Ford promoted in its ads.

History has not treated the 1974 to 1978 Mustang II with respect, but it was a well-designed car that brought with it many innovations, including a new generation of efficient powerplants.

The base engine, a 2.3-liter four-cylinder with a single overhead camshaft and metric components, may not have set the world on fire from a performance aspect, but it replaced Ford's old 200-cubic-inch six-cylinder and remained the Mustang's standard powerplant for 20 years. During development, it was tested thoroughly to meet the company's highest standards for noise, vibration, and harshness (NVH). To encourage trouble-free operation, it received hydraulic valve-lash adjusters—a

1974 HARDTOP

Price: $3,081

Engine: 2.3-liter four-cylinder, 88 horsepower 2.8-liter V-6, 105 horsepower

0–60 mph: 13.8 seconds (Mach 1, 2.8-liter V-6, four-speed, 3.55:1 axle)

Top Speed: 99 mph

unique addition to any OHC engine at that time. Necessary emissions equipment was designed into the engine itself, rather than having it attached later. The 2.3-liter wore a two-barrel carburetor and could be mated to a manual four-speed or extra-cost three-speed automatic.

Ford of Germany produced the 2.8-liter V-6, found in that country's popular,

sporty Mercury Capri, but this $229 option (standard in the Mach 1) brought with it many mechanical problems at first, including faulty engine valves, piston rings, and cooling system. For 1974 to 1975, it was available only with a four-speed manual transmission. *Photos by Jerry Heasley.*

Did You Know?

Of the 385,993 Mustang IIs Ford sold in 1974, 252,470 were the Hardtop and 2+2 base models, suggesting the company had overestimated public demand for its luxurious Ghia notchback and sporty Mach 1. The Ghia outsold the Mach 1 by two to one (more accurately, 89,477 to 44,046).

Still fighting a slow economy and fears of another fuel crisis, Ford produced all four-cylinder Mustang IIs as MPG models for 1976. This designation meant they received a lower 2.79:1 axle ratio and wide-ratio manual transmission for an advertised boost to 34 miles per gallon on the highway.

The hot news for Mustang enthusiasts, though, was the introduction of a Cobra II cosmetic/handling package available only on the 2+2 model for only $325. Engine choice was left to the buyer, so a

1976 COBRA II

Price: $4,106 ('76 2+2 plus Cobra package)
Engine: 2.3-liter four-cylinder, 92 horsepower
2.8-liter V-6, 103 horsepower
5.0-liter V-8, 139 horsepower
0–60 mph: 10.5 seconds (5.0-liter V-8, automatic)
Top Speed: 106 mph (5.0-liter V-8, automatic)

Shelby Mustang–like Cobra II might have an MPG four-cylinder, 2.8-liter six, or 5.0-liter V-8 under the hood. Mimicking Carroll Shelby's 1965 to 1970 Mustang

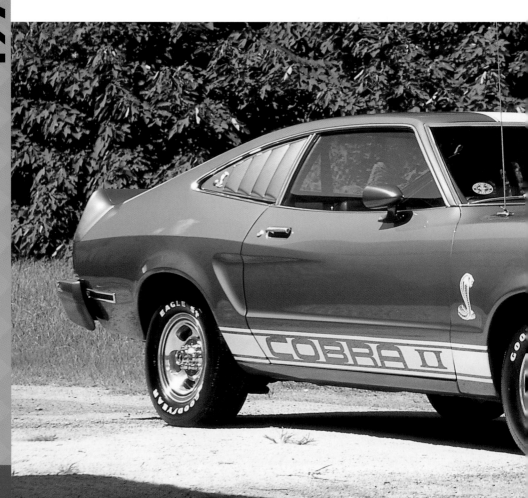

GT-350, the package included racing stripes across the hood, roof, and hatch; a blacked-out grille treatment; color-keyed racing mirrors; rear quarter window louvers; a front air dam; a forward-facing, nonfunctional hood scoop; a rear hatch spoiler; a brushed aluminum instrument panel and door panel appliqués; Cobra insignias on the front fenders; and styled steel wheels wearing steel-belted tires. The Cobra II could be ordered in White (with blue stripes), Blue (white stripes), or Black (gold stripes).

Although he was no longer involved with Ford's product development, Carroll Shelby's likeness appeared in Cobra II magazine ads, as did a photograph of a real GT-350.

Did You Know?

Jim Wangers, who is often described as the "father of the Pontiac GTO," designed and (for 1976 only) installed Cobra II components at a small "Motortown" plant near Ford's Dearborn factory. Ford created Cobra IIs in-house for 1977 and 1978.

The fact that there was a King Cobra package available on the 1978 Mustang proves that Ford was aware of the effect Pontiac's Trans Am had on young performance car buyers. Pontiac's starring role in the previous year's *Smokey and the Bandit* established for a generation the

1978 KING COBRA

Price: $6,350 (includes King Cobra package)
Engine: 5.0-liter V-8, 139 horsepower
0–60 mph: 10.5 seconds est. (5.0-liter V-8, automatic)
Top Speed: 106 mph est. (5.0-liter V-8, automatic)

idea that the hottest car of the 1970s was a 220-horsepower black Trans Am with a screaming Firebird graphic on the hood and a set of T-tops.

Ford wanted in on the action, even though the cosmetic package would be applied to a body in its final year of production.

For $1,277, Ford would add to a 2+2 a unique tape treatment with a giant snake decal on the hood and pinstriping around the hatchback's greenhouse, deck lid, fender lips, rocker panels, belt, roof, and side windows. A cow-catcher of a spoiler rode up front. Each door wore a King Cobra nameplate, as did the rear spoiler, and the standard engine's size was announced in tape on either side of the rear-facing, nonfunctional hood scoop. The King Cobra package also included rear quarter flares, a black grille and moldings, and color-keyed sport mirrors on each door. A coiled Cobra decorated the center cap of each lacy-spoke aluminum wheel, which was dressed with raised white letter tires.

Did You Know?

Only 4,306 buyers drove home in '78 King Cobras, making the one-year-only package a rare sight on today's roads. More people opted for the extra-cost automatic (2,289) over the standard four-speed manual transmission (2,017).

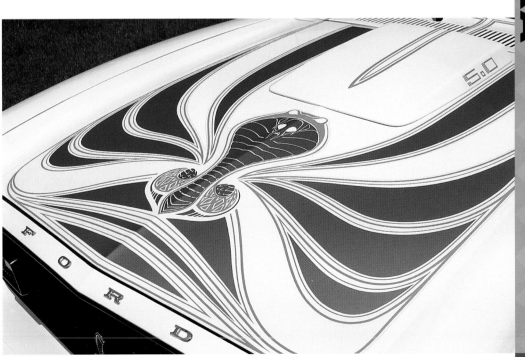

CHAPTER 3
THIRD GENERATION: A FOX IS BORN

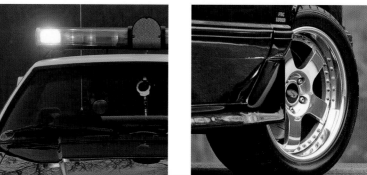

In September 1978, Ford Motor Company introduced its "New Breed" Mustang, whose shape was heavily influenced by European design studios and the wind tunnel. Thanks to such innovations as flush-fitting glass, a smoother nose, and other built-in aerodynamic aids, this third-generation pony car sliced through the wind with a record-low drag coefficient of 0.44 for the hatchback and 0.46 for the coupe.

Lighter steel, thinner glass, and more plastic and aluminum kept the new car's curb weight at a trim 2,600 pounds in base four-cylinder form. With an overall length of 179.1 inches (a four-inch gain over the Mustang II) and a 100.5-inch wheelbase (up from 96.2 inches), the '79 Mustang was larger in every respect than its predecessor, but weighed 200 pounds *less*. It also gained 20 percent more room throughout the passenger compartment.

The '79 model introduced new styling themes, including the Mustang's first rectangular quad-headlamp system, wide taillight lenses that wrapped around the rear quarter panels, and sail-shaped quarter windows. A tall greenhouse made the roomy interior very accommodating for even the largest passengers.

Engines for 1979 were primarily Mustang II carryovers, including the base 88-horsepower, 2.3-liter four-cylinder (now in its sixth year of production); a 109-horsepower, 2.8-liter V-6 (to be replaced, without fanfare, with Ford's ancient 200-cubic-inch inline six-cylinder when German-built V-6 supplies ran low); and a two-barrel 5.0-liter V-8 that chugged out 140 horsepower.

The company began a long but unsuccessful love affair with turbocharging in 1979 when it unveiled a force-fed version of its 2.3-liter four. Brought to market too soon, this high-tech powerplant featured a Garrett AiResearch TO3 turbocharger (limited to 6 psi of boost) and two-barrel carburetor that never worked well together. Burned-out turbines and catastrophic oil leaks were common on the early motors.

Transmission choices were limited to four-speed manuals and three-speed automatics.

Standard MacPherson struts, front disc brakes, rack-and-pinion steering, four-link rear suspension, and an optional handling package built around Michelin TRX radials and metric alloy wheels turned the pony into a real handler. Comparison tests of the time revealed the Mustang could keep up with its more-powerful Camaro/Firebird competition on a road course.

The Mustang was offered in base form or as an upscale Ghia, the latter named for the Italian design studio Ford had owned since 1973. Ghia brought with it many color-keyed components, such as dual remote-control mirrors, quarter louvers, and bodyside molding inserts and many interior luxury upgrades. Both trim levels were available in hatchback or coupe form. Ford added some spice to the Mustang with its pricey ($1,173) Cobra package, which came with the turbocharged engine, special turbo hood scoop, TRX tire/wheel combo, and special handling equipment. The Cobra model, which Ford hoped was the street equivalent of Pontiac's Trans Am, could be had only as a hatchback. (In true Trans Am fashion, a gaudy, coiled-snake hood graphic was available for the Cobra—a $78 option.)

The sporty new Mustang body concealed a humble unit-body platform first seen on 1978 Ford Fairmont and Mercury Zephyr two-door, four-door, and station wagon models. Lincoln-Mercury-Ford engineers knew it as the Fox chassis because the company used Audi/Volkswagen's Fox compact as its target. The platform was so versatile that Ford eventually used it on at least 25 different vehicles, including the Capri, Granada/Versailles, Thunderbird/Cougar, and Lincoln Continental.

Anyone who thinks less of the Fox Mustang for sharing its platform with grocery-getting sedans does not know much about the car's history. The Mustang would never have been born had it not been for Ford's popular but none-too-sexy Falcon, with which it shared major unit-body components and powertrains.

Evolutionary improvements—some minor, some major—gave the Fox Mustang an enviable lifespan of 15 years. The Fox-4, so called because it incorporated several major Fox carryover components, was the foundation for the 1994 Mustang. Only with the introduction of the S197 Mustang in 2005 did the marque fully divest itself of the Fox legacy.

As it had in 1964, Mustang paced the 1979 Indianapolis 500—or, to be more accurate, three identical Mustangs modified by Jack Roush Performance Engineering paced the annual Midwest racing spectacle. Each car's engine incorporated a stock 5.0-liter V-8 block with a Boss 302 crankshaft, 351 Windsor heads, a dual-plane aluminum high-rise intake manifold, and a 600cfm Holley four-barrel carburetor. It has been estimated those massaged V-8s, backed by modified C-4 automatic transmissions,

1979 INDY PACE CAR REPLICA

Price: $9,012
Engine: 2.3-liter turbo four, 131 horsepower
5.0-liter V-8, 140 horsepower
0–60 mph: 8.7 seconds (V-8, four-speed)
9.1 seconds (turbo, four-speed)
Top Speed: 118 mph (V-8, four-speed)
Production: 10,478

produced 280 horsepower. Ford's TRX suspension was lowered one inch to improve handling, and Cars and Concepts

installed T-roofs for greater visibility during the race and parade laps.

This opportunity compelled Ford to release a commemorative line of Indy Pace Car replicas. All Indy hatchbacks were identically decked out in Pewter Metallic with black lower-body trim, orange/red/black striping, a reverse-facing hood scoop, a sunroof, Marchal fog lights, Recaro seats, low-profile Michelin TRX radials, three-spoke metric alloy rims, and a large set of "Official Pace Car" decals that could be installed at the owner's discretion.

Of the 10,478 Pace Car replicas built, 5,970 were turbocharged fours with four-speed manual transmissions; 2,402 were V-8/four-speeds; and 2,106 were V-8/automatics. Ford's Dearborn plant produced 7,634; San Jose, California, built 2,844.

Did You Know?

The sixth and seventh characters in a '79 Mustang must be "48" for the car to be a true Pace Car replica. Enthusiasts considered the Pace Car replicas to be instant collectibles and put many of them in storage with their plastic seat covers and factory OK stickers still in place.

The Mustang experienced a performance renaissance when Ford offered it with an improved 5.0-liter V-8 and four-speed manual transmission in 1982. "The Boss is Back!" touted the company's ads, although the V-8's large Motorcraft two-barrel carburetor and 157-horsepower output made it only a shadow of the 1969 and 1970 Boss 302/429 and 1971 Boss 351. Still, when compared to that year's redesigned, 400-pound-heavier Camaro/Firebird, the

1982 GT

Price: $8,308

Engine: 5.0-liter V-8, 157 horsepower
4.2-liter V-8, 120 horsepower

0–60 mph: 8 seconds (5.0-liter, four-speed)

Top Speed: 118 mph (5.0-liter, four-speed)

Production: 23,447

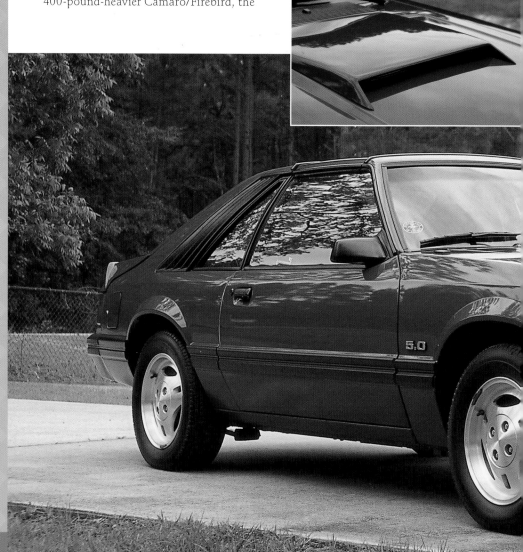

Mustang produced the fastest acceleration times in its class.

The high-output (HO) 5.0-liter V-8 could be ordered with the hatchback or coupe body style in a variety of trim levels, but it was the look-at-me, hatchback-only GT package that made us all remember how awesome Ford's pony could be. With a sticker price of $8,308, the GT replaced the 1979 to 1981 Cobra and wore 14-inch cast-aluminum wheels, front and rear spoilers, fog lamps, blackout trim treatment, luxury seats, and a console. The closed-off hood scoop did not draw air into the engine, but it did allow clearance for a high-flow air cleaner. Going nuts with the order form could push the top Mustang above the $10,000 mark with popular options, such as TRX suspension ($105), Recaro seats ($834), T-roof ($1,021), and air conditioning ($676).

Did You Know?

The GT has been part of the Mustang line from 1964 to present, except during 1970 to 1981, when it was replaced by the Mach 1 and Cobra. Ford's HO 5.0-liter was only available with a four-speed manual during 1982 and 1983; to order a GT with an automatic, a buyer had to take a 120-horsepower 4.2-liter V-8.

Mustangers had much reason to rejoice in 1984. The number of available engines, body styles, transmissions, and trim levels had not been this high since the performance proliferation of 1969. Six engines—two of which were turbocharged four-cylinders—ranged from 88 to 175 horsepower. With the introduction the previous year of a true convertible, the Mustang line had three attractive bodies from which to choose. HO V-8 Mustangs could be ordered with

1984 GT-350

Price: $427 plus Mustang GT (for 41A package)
Engine: 2.3-liter turbo four, five-speed, 145 horsepower
5.0-liter V-8, AOD, 165 horsepower
5.0-liter V-8, five-speed, 175 horsepower
0–60 mph: 6.86 seconds (5.0-liter, five-speed)
Top Speed: 129.6 mph (5.0-liter, five-speed)
Production: 5,260

five-speed overdrive transmissions. The marque had come a long way since the dark days of the 1970s.

Because 1984 was the Mustang's 20th anniversary, Ford celebrated with a limited-edition package that could be ordered with either its GT (V-8) or Turbo GT (four-cylinder) models, which were available only in hatchback and convertible body styles. The 41A option required Oxford White paint (plus vintage-style running horse fender badges; racing stripes; color-keyed bumpers, grille, and rub strip; and narrow body molding) and a Canyon Red interior.

Of the 5,260 commemorative GT-350s produced, 3,333 were V-8 hatchbacks; 1,213 were V-8 convertibles; 350 were turbo hatchbacks; and only 104 were turbocharged four-cylinder convertibles. The rest were VIP convertibles and Canadian export models. All but the VIP cars were produced between March 5 and March 22, 1984.

Did You Know?

Carroll Shelby, who produced the original GT-350 Mustang from 1965 to 1970, sued Ford Motor Company for using what he felt was a protected name on the '84 anniversary cars. He eventually lost the suit when the decision was made that the name had reverted to public domain from lack of use.

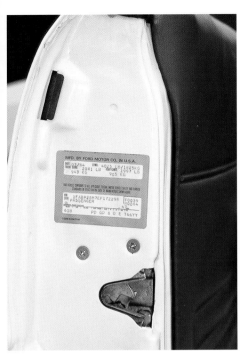

Steve Saleen was a business school graduate and Sports Car Club of America Formula Atlantic and Trans-Am series racer in the early 1980s when he introduced a high-performance version of Ford's Mustang. That first Saleen Mustang was a borrowed white hatchback with a V-8 and five-speed manual transmission, to which Steve added his Racecraft suspension components (specific-rate front and rear springs, Bilstein

1984 SALEEN

Price: $14,300
Engine: 5.0-liter V-8, 175 horsepower
0–60 mph: 6.5 seconds (est.)
Top Speed: 130 mph (est.)
Production: 3

pressurized struts and shocks, a front chassis brace, and urethane bushings), 15-inch Goodyear Eagle GTs, Hayashi alloy wheels,

an aerodynamic package, and interior upgrades, such as a Wolf Racing steering wheel and Saleen gauges.

The only option offered was a Sanyo AM/FM stereo cassette system with upgraded speakers.

Because it was nearly impossible to legally sell a car with a modified powerplant in 1984, Saleen's only engine upgrade was a simple Cal Custom chromed air cleaner lid over the stock Ford four-barrel carburetor. The Petaluma, California–based Saleen Autosport only built three cars that first year, owing to a late start in the season, but 1985 sales jumped to 140 units.

After a couple of years generating publicity for Saleen Autosport, that first Saleen Mustang was returned to its original owner, Robyn Lee Saleen—Steve's sister.

Did You Know?

Saleen Mustangs have carried unique serial numbers since the first one was produced in 1984. Eager to give the impression that his enterprise was already successful, Steve Saleen assigned his first car the serial number 84-0032, suggesting it was the 32nd car to bear his name. The trick must have worked.

In 1984, Ford Motor Company tried once again to make the American driving enthusiast love turbochargers when it introduced its world-class SVO Mustang.

Unlike the sad, wheezy, carbureted turbo engines Ford sold from 1979 to 1981, the SVO engine was a fully evolved powerplant whose computer programming married fuel injection to a modified four-cylinder for an impressive 175-horsepower output.

The good news was not limited to the engine compartment. Standard SVO

1984 - 1986 SVO

Price: $15,596 (1984)
$14,521 (1985)
$15,272 (1986)
Engine: 2.3-liter turbo four, 175 horsepower (1984–85)
2.3-liter turbo four, 205 horsepower (1985.5)
2.3-liter turbo four, 200 horsepower (1986)
0–60 mph: 7.5 seconds (1984)
Top Speed: 134 mph (1984)
Production: 4,508 (1984)
1,954 (1985)
3,382 (1986)

equipment included a Borg-Warner T-5 five-speed manual transmission with a Hurst shifter, four-wheel disc brakes, Koni adjustable gas-filled shocks, 16-inch Goodyear NCT tires, cast-aluminum wheels, and a functional hood scoop—the first such scoop on a Mustang since the 1973 Dual Ram option. The interior sported multiadjustable, articulated leather bucket seats; a switch for operating the suspension's three settings; and a fat, leather-covered steering wheel.

Although built on a standard Mustang Fox body, the SVO wore a different front cap (with recessed headlights) and a bi-level rear wing that could be swapped for a single wing upon ordering.

So, why did the SVO only last three years? The magazines and enthusiasts loved the high-tech pony, but it cost twice as much as a base four-cylinder and nearly $6,000 more than the comparable V-8 GT.

Did You Know?

The SVO Mustang was developed to recapture American car buyers who had been seduced by sophisticated European sedans. One test drive made it clear the SVO engineering team was made up of experienced high-performance drivers. An example of their racetrack mentality is the arrangement of control pedals that allowed heel-toe flexibility.

In only four years since its return to the Mustang lineup, the 5.0-liter V-8 climbed from 157 to 210 horsepower. Ford engineers were getting better every season at finding power in the 5.0-liter HO powerplant. For 1985, those gains came through the use of low-friction roller tappets, a high-performance camshaft, stainless-steel headers, twin pipes, and a new accessory drive system.

The year 1985 also marked the 15th anniversary of a popular Kansas City, Missouri, sales promotion in which 96 Mach 1 Mustangs were ordered with

1985 TWISTER II

Price: $9,885 (GT hatchback)
Engine: 5.0-liter V-8, 210 horsepower (manual transmission)
5.0-liter V-8, 165 horsepower (automatic transmission)
0–60 mph: 6.4 seconds (5.0-liter V-8, five-speed)
Top Speed: 135 mph (5.0-liter V-8, five-speed)
Production: 90 (Twister II)

Grabber Orange paint and tornado-like twister graphics. To commemorate the occasion, the KC dealer network ordered—with Ford's cooperation—90 5.0-liter GT

Mustangs in Jalapeno Red, Medium Canyon Red Metallic, Oxford White, and Silver Metallic and sold them as Twister II models.

The Twister II was no different from a stock GT, but it came with updated tornado graphics, a dash plaque, a commemorative coaster, and a Ford press kit about the vehicle. Of the 90 produced, 74 were hatchbacks with five-speed manual transmissions; 9 were convertibles with five-speeds; 5 were convertible models with automatic transmissions; and only 2 were convertible five-speed cars.

In 2008 and 2009, R&A Motorsports, of Lee's Summit, Missouri, revisited the theme with 17 special editions (13 coupes, 4 convertibles) known as Twister Specials.

Did You Know?

For the second year in a row, Ford offered an automatic transmission with the 5.0-liter V-8. Unfortunately, the auto tranny came attached to a less-powerful version of the 5.0-liter in 1984 and 1985 that produced only 165 horsepower. The five-speed engine wore a Holley four-barrel carburetor; the auto trans version was fed by electronic fuel injection.

In 1987, a thorough facelift and more engine improvements to the 5.0-liter V-8 turned the Fox Mustang into a product so perfect that Ford dared not change it substantially for the next *seven years*. After a drop in output the previous year, due to an inefficient head design, the HO jumped to 225 horsepower, which, for the time, made it one of the most-affordable performance cars on the market.

Even the base 2.3-liter four-cylinder was improved for 1987. With the addition of a

1987 GT

Price: $15,724 (GT convertible)
Engine: 5.0-liter V-8, 225 horsepower
0–60 mph: 6.3 seconds (5.0-liter, five-speed, 3.08:1 axle)
Top Speed: 137 mph (5.0-liter, five-speed, 3.08:1 axle)

multiport fuel-injection system, the sturdy miser received a boost to 90 horsepower.

Ordering a Mustang was now greatly simplified. The four and V-8 would be the only engine choices through 1994, as the V-6 and turbocharged SVOs were both dropped this year. Each was available with either a five-speed manual or four-speed automatic overdrive. Ford continued to offer the hatchback, two-door coupe, and convertible body styles.

From 1982 to 1986, the GT package had been nothing more than a stripe, fake hood scoop, and foglights, with the same V-8 that could be ordered in the base Mustang. The 1987 to 1993 GT still shared its HO with the cheaper LX, but it gained distinctive aerodynamic components, a 15-inch turbine wheel design, and louvered taillight lenses that set it apart from the herd.

Did You Know?

Horsepower ratings are never exact, no matter the company reporting them. For 1987 only, V-8 Mustangs with automatic transmissions wore restrictive mufflers to meet noise standards, resulting in an unadvertised five-horsepower deficit. A camshaft modification in 1988 took away three horsepower, but this was not reflected in the official rating.

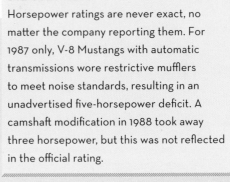

Steve Saleen benefited from the enormous amount of money and engineering time Ford invested in the 1987 Fox Mustang because it gave him a vastly improved product on which to build his high-performance cars.

For 1987, Saleen introduced many innovations to his lineup that would not be available on Ford's Mustangs for many years. Four-wheel disc brakes became standard equipment, as did FloFit seats, 16-inch alloy wheels, and many chassis

1989 SALEEN SSC

Price: $36,500
Engine: 5.0-liter V-8, 290 horsepower
0–60 mph: 5.9 seconds
Top Speed: n/a
Production: 161

components that served to stiffen the somewhat flexible Fox platform. All these improvements aided—and were inspired

by—Saleen's racing efforts, which resulted in Saleen Autosport clinching four SCCA championships in 1987.

In 1989, after hiring a former official from the Environmental Protection Agency, Saleen certified for sale in 50 states a 290-horsepower version of the 5.0-liter engine. Rather than offer it as an optional powerplant, Saleen created the SSC, which took the Saleen Mustang concept to a higher level. The SSC came standard with an onboard adjustable suspension, Auburn rear axle gears, an all-leather interior, a two-seater format, a high-end stereo, and a unique white-only paint scheme.

Did You Know?

The SSC concept was born in 1988 when Saleen put together a special model to celebrate his company's fifth year in business. The one-off SA-5 was, in essence, a black SSC prototype and test mule. When an automotive writer told Saleen that black cars seldom appear on magazine covers, he changed the color scheme.

Saleen's 1989 SSC was intended to be a one-year-only limited edition, but its improved, certified 5.0-liter continued the next four years as the basis for another ultimate Mustang—the SC. Like the SSC, the SC was offered only as a hatchback from 1990 to 1992, but Saleen made a convertible available during its final year of 1993.

   The SC was equipped in much the same style as the SSC, including the earlier car's five-spoke, 16-inch alloy DP wheels; heavy-duty Borg-Warner T-5 five-speed;

1990 – 1993 SALEEN SC

Price: $33,990 (1990)
$34,750 (1991)
$39,990 (1993)
Engine: 5.0-liter V-8, 304 horsepower (1990–91)
5.0-liter V-8, supercharged, 450 horsepower (1993)
Production: 13 (1990)
10 (1991)
5, inc. three convertibles (1993)

Auburn-built 3.55:1 rear gears; and enhanced Racecraft suspension. A new Saleen-cast upper and lower intake manifold and stainless-steel headers boosted the V-8 to 304 horsepower for 1990.

Monroe's adjustable suspension became an extra-cost option, as did the interior chassis reinforcement (also known as a roll bar). The SC, like the standard Saleen Mustang, could seat four because Saleen did not see fit to carry over the two-seater layout and heavy rear sound enclosure to the SC.

SCs were available in Black, White, or Bright Red for 1990; Saleen added Twilight Blue Metallic to the list for 1991. With sales of the aging Fox Mustang declining, Saleen produced only 17 cars in 1992, none of which were SCs. For 1993, the SC's final year, color choices were limited only by Ford's order form.

Did You Know?

Saleen Mustangs came with Stern three-piece, 17-inch alloy wheels in 1992, two years before Ford offered that diameter on its GT. In 1993, due to supply problems, Saleen Mustangs and SCs were equipped with rims from Stern, Logic, and Speedline. The final Fox-body Saleen was an SC convertible that shipped on April 13, 1994.

The story of Mustang cop cars goes back to 1982, when Ford Motor Company outbid Chevrolet to supply the California Highway Patrol with Mustangs instead of Camaros. Those 1982 L-series notchbacks with 157-horsepower V-8s were necessary in that state because its wide-open freeways and large population of expensive, high-powered imports put law enforcement officers at a disadvantage during pursuit. Ford's bid set a price that year of $6,868 per car, in base form.

1992 SPECIAL SERVICE VEHICLE

Price: The revenue from about 100 speeding tickets
Engine: Same as your '92 GT
0–60 mph: That's five over the limit, son.
Top Speed: Just try me.

Contrary to popular mythology, the California Highway Patrol's Mustangs were not sporting hopped-up, blueprinted 5.0-liters with special cams or (with later

models) top-secret computer chips. From the first 1982 to the last 1993—about 15,000 cars in all—the Special Service Vehicles were bone-stock Mustangs with modifications performed only in the interest of greater durability or comfort. Even had the police, highway patrol, and other U.S. enforcement bodies requested more horsepower, the cost of certifying engine changes and keeping enough spare parts available for maintenance and repairs would have pushed the cop specials into a higher price category.

Changes to these police interceptors and pursuit vehicles usually involved such mundane equipment as calibrated speedometers, transmission coolers, a deleted underhood sound absorber, reinforced driver seat mounts, and blue silicone, high-temperature hoses.

Did You Know?

Mustang enthusiasts seeking the least-expensive performance models tried to purchase new Fox-body police interceptors from their dealerships but were turned down. On rare occasion, however, a pursuit-spec Mustang would be refused after delivery or receive minor cosmetic damage, leaving it free to be sold to the general public.

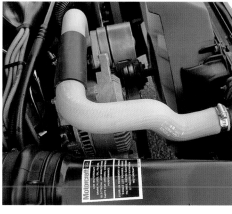

Steeda is a combination of the first names of business partners Steve Chicisola and Dario Orlando, the founders of Steeda Autosports. Orlando's grandfather and father worked for Ford Motor Company, which may explain why the import-car shop owner and apparel entrepreneur began developing high-performance Mustang parts in 1988.

The company's first products included new designs for strut tower braces and

1992 STEEDA

Price: $14,207 (5.0-liter hatchback, not including Steeda conversion)
Engine: 5.0-liter V-8, 300 horsepower
0–60 mph: 5.9 seconds (est.)
Top Speed: 150 mph (est.)

subframe connectors—two items Fox Mustang owners needed to limit chassis flex. When Orlando felt he had made serious

improvements in the Mustang's handling on a race course, he began offering turnkey cars for sale. To identify the Mustangs with his adopted home in Florida, Orlando planned to call them Sebrings (for the road course in that state) but, instead, took his lawyer's advice and adopted the name of his and Chicisola's apparel business.

As Steeda's reputation for designing new parts grew, Ford Motor Company asked Orlando to bring one of his modified Mustangs to the Naples, Florida, proving grounds, where engineers spent all day evaluating the car's improvements.

They must have liked what they drove because Steeda is now the world's largest manufacturer of aftermarket parts for Ford.

Did You Know?

Steeda holds more than 40 patents applicable to Ford performance parts. That list includes a charge motion delete kit, its Tri-Ax shifter, and aluminum control arms. Steeda was the first company to work with Ford through the SEMA Technology Transfer initiative on its engine management and calibration specs.

After 14 years of production, the Fox-body Mustang's retirement was long overdue. Sales had declined from 1987, when a quarter-of-a-million Mustangs went to new homes, to 1992, when Ford sold fewer than 80,000 units. When the Fox platform debuted in 1979, no one could predict the same chassis would carry Ford's performance flag well into the 1990s, but there it was. Adding to the impression of old age, the basic design of the Mustang's "Windsor" pushrod V-8 engine had been in production for more than 30 years.

A new body (with only a few carried-over Fox parts) was slated to debut in 1994, and the corporate modular V-8 was scheduled for the 1996 Mustang, but these promises of good things to come would not sell cars in the short run.

To boost the Mustang's image for model-year 1993, Ford's Special Vehicle Engineering (SVE) and Special Vehicle Team

(SVT) announced a limited run of factory-blessed supercars that would outrun Chevrolet's Camaro or Pontiac's Firebird. The Camaro-killer turned out to be a pair of 235-horsepower V-8 hatchbacks boldly called Cobra and Cobra R. Reviving the coiled-snake emblem—defanged by several pretend muscle cars in the 1970s and early 1980s—suggested that Ford would not settle for second place in the market or the track.

1993 COBRA AND COBRA R

Price: $18,205 (Cobra)
$25,692 (Cobra R)
Engine: 5.0-liter V-8, 235 horsepower
0–60 mph: 5.7 seconds (Cobra)
5.5 seconds (Cobra R)
Top Speed: 150 mph
Production: 4,993 (Cobra)
107 (Cobra R)

Did You Know?

The '93 Cobra closely followed the recipe of the failed 1984 to 1986 SVO Mustang, but with one major exception—there was a V-8 under the hood. In its first two years, the Cobra surpassed the earlier SVO's sales numbers by nearly 2,000 cars.

CHAPTER 4
FOURTH GENERATION: AFTER THE FOX

Ford Motor Company gave the best present possible to Mustang enthusiasts for the popular marque's 30th birthday in 1994—an all-new Mustang! Well, to be truthful, the car did have 500 carried-over Fox components, such as the powertrain, floorpans, and brackets tucked out of sight, but a stylish new body made everyone forget that its squarish predecessor had stayed on the market several years too long.

Ford's Team Mustang introduced the 1994 model on October 15, 1993, after spending three years in an old Montgomery Ward warehouse south of Dearborn. The new Mustang featured squinting aerodynamic headlights on either side of a curved grille opening and a body entirely free of sharp edges. The melted-soap styling was attractive, but not aggressively so. It was designed to offend no one, and many cues from the past (such as the long-hood/short-deck profile, functional side vents, and three-element taillights) endeared the car to a new generation of enthusiasts. Considering the group was given a limited budget, it is remarkable that the 1994 model looks so radically different from the 1993 version.

Team Mustang was given a mandate to eradicate the body flex and noise problems inherent in the Fox chassis. The final product, which was known internally as the SN-95, surpassed its rigidity goals, registering an 80 percent improvement in the convertible's chassis torsion and a 44 percent increase in the closed model. New technologies contributed to the stiffness, including bonding the front and rear glass to their frames with a rigid urethane glue and making thicker rocker panels and roof rails. The new car also met upcoming federal crash standards that required slamming a 3,000-pound test sled into the vehicle's side at 33 miles per hour.

At 181.5 inches from bumper to bumper, the SN-95 was 2.4 inches longer than the Fox had been when it debuted in 1979. The wheelbase of 101.3 inches was a 0.9-inch stretch. Width grew by 2.8 inches to 71.9, and the new roofline was 1.4 inches higher at 52.9 inches.

As of 1994, the Mustang would no longer be available as a notchback, hatchback, and convertible. Instead, Ford created a coupe whose sporty greenhouse suggested a fastback roof—similar to what the original 2+2 had in 1965—and developed a convertible from that platform. Tuning noise, vibration, and harshness out of the ragtop's body meant installing a 25-pound mass damper inside the right front fender well.

Ford hoped to rekindle the kind of Mustang fervor that had led to near-riots at dealerships in 1964, and its advertising drew direct comparisons to the original model. Magazine ads claimed,

"It is what it was." Hundreds of thousands of posters and cards were distributed at car shows displaying a new convertible pony alongside a 1965 droptop. Ford's marketers worked hand-in-hand with the Mustang Club of America and similar organizations to ensure that vintage Mustang collectors, restorers, and modifiers had every chance to fall in love again.

Dropping the complex multilevel trim packages of the past, Ford offered the 1994 with two body styles, two engine choices (V-6 and V-8), two transmissions (five-speed manual and four-speed automatic), 11 exterior colors (including Canary

Yellow, three shades of red, Bright Blue, and Deep Forest Green), and five interior colors. The V-6 cars were known simply as Mustangs; V-8 models were exclusively Mustang GTs. Prices for the latest version of this American icon were reasonable—$13,355 for the base coupe and $20,150 in convertible form. Moving up to the GT level meant paying $17,270 for a coupe and $21,960 for a convertible.

The standard equipment list was longer than ever. It included dual, electric, remote-control mirrors; four-speaker stereo; air bags for driver and passenger; console with arm rest; driver-side foot rest; full instrumentation; dual visor mirrors; four-way powered driver's seat; tilt steering; side window demisters; an extensive Light Group package; and reclining cloth bucket seats with head restraints. Convertibles featured power retractable tops with protective covers, illuminated visor mirrors, power deck lid release, glass backlight, and power door locks and windows.

In spite of what the advertisements said, in terms of creature comforts, the new base Mustang was much better outfitted than buyers of the 1965 model could have dreamed.

FOURTH GENERATION: AFTER THE FOX

Mustang engine choices changed slightly for 1994. The four-cylinder—essentially the same 2.3-liter plant introduced in the 1974 Mustang II—was dropped. Base Mustangs received a version of the same 3.8-liter, 145-horsepower V-6 that had been pulling heavier Taurus, Thunderbird, and Lincoln Continental models for several years, giving the cheapest pony a 38 percent increase in power. The 5.0-liter V-8—a Mustang staple since 1968—received a minor boost to 215

1994 GT
Price: $13,355 (base)
$17,270 (GT)
Engine: 5.0-liter V-8, 215 horsepower
0–60 mph: 6.7 seconds (GT)
Top Speed: 140 mph (GT)

horsepower at 4,200 rpm by way of a low-profile intake manifold and hypereutectic aluminum alloy pistons.

Rolling stock was improved with the SN-95 design. Base V-6 Mustangs wore 15-inch steel wheels with plastic covers and 205/65-15 all-season black sidewall Goodyear Eagle GA tires. For a few extra bucks, those same Goodyears could be fitted to three-spoke alloy wheels. GT rims were five-spoke, 16-inch designs wearing 225/55-16 Firestone Firehawk rubber, or buyers could upgrade to three-spoke 17-inchers with wide 245/45-17 Goodyear Eagle GTs.

For the first time in Mustang history, all models received four-wheel disc brakes. An anti-lock brake system was optional.

Although sales of the 1994 were nowhere near that of the '65 model, Ford happily pumped out 123,198 of the new Mustangs. The most popular configuration was the V-6 coupe, at 42,883 units.

Did You Know?

Of the SN-95's 1,850 parts, 1,330 were new. To demonstrate how little the '94 Mustang shared with the '93, Ford mounted a stripped '94 chassis on a rotisserie with color-coded parts indicating carryover components. This "Mustang on a spit" was displayed at car shows around the country.

DRIVER WINDOW control.
• Tap for express down
  or
• Push and hold until window
  reaches desired opening.

Ford's in-house tuner, the Special Vehicle Team, produced hopped-up Cobra coupes and convertibles based on the new-for-1994 Mustang.

The centerpiece of the premium-performance model was a 240-horsepower version of the Mustang GT's 5.0-liter V-8. The additional power was the result of computer tweaking and a taller Thunderbird intake manifold (made possible by deleting the GT's strut-tower-to-cowl brace). All Cobras were fitted with Borg-Warner T5 five-speed manual transmissions.

1994 SVT COBRA

Price: $20,765 (coupe)
$26,845 (convertible)
Engine: 5.0-liter V-8, 235 horsepower
0–60 mph: 6.9 seconds (convertible)
Top Speed: 140 mph (convertible)
Production: 5,009 (coupe)
1,000 (convertible)

Cobras were not easily mistaken for standard Mustangs, thanks to unique cosmetic upgrades, such as a front bumper fascia incorporating round auxiliary lights,

European-style reflector headlights, and numerous coiled-snake emblems. The Cobra brand made itself known in the passenger compartment as well, with a Cobra-specific steering wheel, floor mats, and white-faced gauges.

As it had done the previous year, SVT set up its Cobra suspension with softer springs than those on the GT—400 pounds/inch in front and 160 in the rear. For braking power, SVT applied 13-inch vented discs in front with twin-piston calipers and vented rears measuring 11.65 inches in diameter. All '94

Cobras received Bosch's three-channel, four-sensor ABS system as standard equipment. The new Cobra wore the largest tires in Mustang history—255/45-17 Goodyear Eagle GS-Cs on five-spoke, 17x8-inch alloy rims.

Did You Know?

Not surprisingly, the Mustang was chosen to pace the 1994 Indianapolis 500. Jack Roush modified three Cobra convertibles for race duty, and Ford produced 1,000 Rio Red replicas with saddle leather interiors and saddle tops. Decals were shipped to the dealers inside the cars and left to the buyer's discretion to install them.

The Saleen S-351 transformed Ford's new Mustang coupes and convertibles into Corvette killers. The centerpiece of the S-351 was a stock 351-cubic-inch SVT Lightning V-8 block, to which Saleen engineers added Edelbrock aluminum heads, a roller camshaft and lifters, 65-millimeter throttle body, 77-millimeter mass air sensor, and an EEC-IV engine management system to produce 371 horsepower. A heavy-duty

1994 SALEEN S-351

Price: $34,990 (S-351 coupe)
$40,990 (S-351 convertible)
$45,990 (SR)
Engine: 351-cid V-8, 371 horsepower
351-cid V-8, 480 horsepower
0–60 mph: 5.9 seconds (S-351 coupe)
Top Speed: 170 mph (S-351 coupe)
Production: 44 (S-351)
2 (SR)

Tremec five-speed transmission and 3.27:1 rear gears completed the standard performance package. Saleen offered a Vortech supercharger late in the 1994 season, which boosted the S-351 to a staggering 480 horsepower.

With its redesigned front and rear fascia, Racecraft suspension system, BFGoodrich Comp T/A radials on 18-inch Speedline magnesium wheels, Recaro sport seats, and unique aerodynamic package, the S-351 had the highest level of Saleen-specific equipment to date, and the crew spent 120 man-hours making the conversion.

A super-rare SR model, available only in coupe form, came standard with the supercharged engine and competition-grade suspension and brakes. Even the interior was built for the track, with a four-point roll bar, safety harnesses, and racing Recaro seats trimmed in cloth. The SR was a homologation model intended to get Saleen into Sports Car Club of America competition. In spite of its larger engine, the SR—at 3,094 pounds—weighed substantially less than a stock Mustang GT.

Did You Know?
Saleen debuted its S-351 and SR models (along with a V-6 Sport by Steve Saleen) during the Mustang's 30th anniversary show at Charlotte (North Carolina) Motor Speedway in April of 1994. Also attending the show was a Mustang fan from Arkansas, U.S. President Bill Clinton.

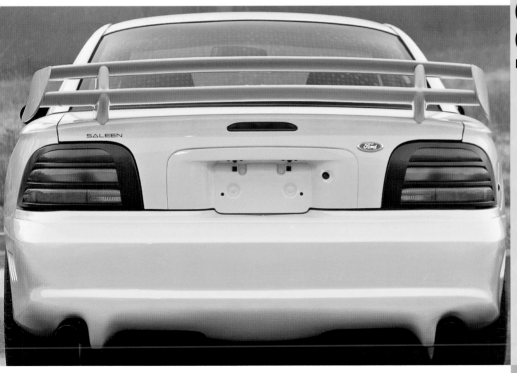

SVT flexed its muscles again in 1995 with a second competition-ready R model Cobra.

While its standard '95 Cobra won fans with a 240-horsepower, 5.0-liter V-8, SVT took the R to a new level by squeezing a 300-horsepower, 5.8-liter (351-cubic-inch) under its uniquely domed fiberglass hood.

1995 SVT COBRA R

Price: $35,499
Engine: 351-cid V-8, 300 horsepower
0–60 mph: 5.2 seconds
Top Speed: 152 mph
Production: 250

This marked the first (and last) time in 21 years a factory-built Mustang was equipped with a 351. The special engine started with a Ford marine block, to which the company added a special cam, aluminum alloy pistons, GT40 heads and lower intake, and a specially designed upper intake manifold.

SVT installed a heavy-duty Tremec five-speed manual transmission and 3.27:1 rear axle gears to augment the R's acceleration. Since it was intended for use on the racetrack, the R was stripped of unnecessary weight, including the air-conditioner, radio, power windows and locks, rear seat, soundproofing materials, and fog lamps. The suspension was enhanced with Eibach springs, Koni adjustable shocks, firmer bushings than the street Cobra used, and five-spoke wheels measuring 17x9 inches with 255/45-17 BFGoodrich Comp T/A radials. SVT pulled the stock gas tank and installed a 20-gallon racing fuel cell.

All '95 Cobra Rs were dressed in Crystal White paint with saddle cloth interiors.

Did You Know?

Ford tried to keep the '95 Cobra R on the track and away from speculators by requiring that all 250 copies be sold to holders of competition licenses granted by SCCA, NHRA, IMSA, IHRA, and other sanctioning bodies. Considering how many no-mile examples have been spotted at auctions and for sale online, their attempt was not entirely successful.

The year 1996 marked a massive change for late-model Mustang powerplants. Ford's Mustang GT lost its beloved 5.0-liter pushrod engine and gained a 4.6-liter V-8 with single overhead camshafts. The 4.6 was down 31 cubic inches from its predecessor, but it matched the outgoing 5.0-liter's 215 horsepower.

With the SVT, the pushrod design was replaced with a 305-horsepower, 4.6-liter with *double* overhead camshafts that had been serving the Lincoln line for

1996 SVT COBRA

Price: $24,810 (coupe)
$27,580 (convertible)
Engine: 4.6-liter DOHC, 305 horsepower
0–60 mph: 5.9 seconds (coupe)
Top Speed: 152 mph (coupe)
Production: 10,006

several years. Its block was cast by the Teksid company in Italy, then shipped to Ford's Romeo, Michigan, plant where it was assembled with four-valve heads,

twin 57-millimeter throttle bodies, and a German-built crankshaft. Cobra motors were handbuilt by 12 two-person teams on the Niche Line, and each received a personally autographed metallic plate on the passenger-side camshaft cover. The Cobra's DOHC setup made the engine physically taller, which required a special domed hood for clearance.

Borg-Warner's new T-45 five-speed manual transmission served in both the Mustang GT and Cobra, although many enthusiastic SVT owners experienced reliability problems with shift forks and synchronizer gears.

Strangely, SVT downsized its Cobra tires for 1996, dropping to a 245/45-17 from the previous year's 255/45-17. The new tire/wheel combo weighed one pound less, creating lower unsprung weight.

Did You Know?

SVT's most popular Cobra color for 1996 was Black (3,175 cars). Its least-ordered color was Crystal White (1,929). The Cobra was also available in Mystic—a scheme developed by GAF that changed from green, purple, blue, or black, depending on angle and intensity of light. The $815 option sold to 1,999 coupe buyers.

Steve Saleen's S-351 was an exciting performance machine, but its super-high price was pushing Saleen faithful away from the brand. In 1996, coinciding with Ford's introduction of the 4.6-liter V-8 to its Mustang line, Saleen created the S-281—essentially the S-351 suspension and body wrapped around a Mustang GT. At an entry-level price below $30,000, it was the most affordable Saleen in three years.

Called S-281 after its engine displacement, it featured massive 245/40-18 BFGoodrich

1996 SALEEN S-281

Price: $28,990 (coupe)
$33,500 (convertible)
Engine: 4.6-liter SOHC, 215 horsepower
0–60 mph: 6.8 seconds (est.)
Top Speed: 140 mph (est)
Production: 438

rubber on 18-inch, five-spoke alloy wheels. For those wanting to pay for more goodies, Saleen offered 18-inch magnesium wheels, Recaro seats, a carbon-fiber hood, 3.55:1 rear

axle gears, and the Speedster package—a hard tonneau cover for the back seat of a convertible and a two-point padded roll bar.

Acknowledging its fan base, Saleen included one-year memberships in the Mustang Club of America and the Saleen Owners & Enthusiasts Club with the purchase of an S-281. The company sold more '96 S-281s than it had any other single model in the previous six years. Even the Budget rental car company purchased 30 S-281 convertibles to use at its premium locations.

Did You Know?

When customers requested it, Saleen would build one of its S-281 coupes or convertibles on an SVT Cobra platform. The program was not advertised, but many enthusiasts felt that combining the Saleen body and suspension with SVT's DOHC engine made the perfect Mustang package. Only 11 such Saleen Cobras were built in 1996.

"This Horse Is Rocking," read the Mustang ads for 1998. Ford made only minor changes to its successful formula, such as the inclusion of polished aluminum wheels, a premium sound system with cassette and CD capability (standard on base coupe and convertible), and Ford's SecuriLock anti-theft system.

Two new option packages were available to buyers: the $595 GT Sport Group (including 17-inch aluminum wheels, striping on hood and fenders, a leather-wrapped shift knob, and an engine oil

1998
Price: $15,970 (coupe)
$20,470 (convertible)
$19,970 (GT coupe)
$23,970 (GT convertible)
Engine: 3.8-liter V-6, 150 horsepower
4.6-liter V-8, 225 horsepower
0–60 mph: 6.8 seconds (GT)
Top Speed: 140 mph (GT)

cooler) and the $345 V-6 Sport Appearance Group (with 16-inch cast-aluminum wheels, a rear spoiler, a leather-wrapped steering wheel, and a lower body accent stripe), which was available on base models only.

It should be noted the 4.6-liter SOHC V-8 gained 10 horsepower for 1998 to achieve a rating of 225. This boost was not enough to put the stock GT in the same performance ballpark as GM's Pontiac Firebird and Chevrolet Camaro, each of whose 5.7-liter V-8s was packing 275 horsepower managed by Corvette-sourced six-speed Borg-Warner T-56 manual transmissions. (The Mustang made do just fine with Borg-Warner's T-45 five-speed.) For a real kick in the pants, Ford enthusiasts had to step up to SVT's Cobra, with its 305-horsepower DOHC 4.6-liter V-8.

Did You Know?

Mustangs with four-speed automatic transmissions were considered low emission vehicles (LEV) in California, New York, Massachusetts, and Connecticut—four states with very stringent standards—in 1998. Mustang popularity increased this model year, with 175,522 ponies going to new homes.

After five years with essentially the same body, the Mustang received a facelift and tummy tuck just in time for its 35th birthday. Ford replaced the rounded-off 1994 to 1998 body with a New Edge design that aggressively sported straight lines and strong creases. The sides were more vertical than before. The tallest scoop (nonfunctional) ever fitted to a Mustang appeared just behind the door, and the GT was given a simulated recessed scoop that resembled the 1968 Mustang's 428 Cobra

1999

Price: $16,470 (coupe)
$21,070 (convertible)
$20,870 (GT coupe)
$24,870 (GT convertible)
Engine: 3.8-liter V-6, 190 horsepower
4.6-liter V-8, 260 horsepower
0–60 mph: 5.4 seconds (GT)
Top Speed: 140 mph (GT)

Jet air intake. Dual exhaust tips grew to three inches in diameter.

Changes were not cosmetic only—Ford was quick to show off the new car's engineering improvements, such as the revised floorpan sealing and foam-packed rocker panels that reduced road noise. Subframe connectors cut down on the convertible's mid-car shake. Weight was reduced everywhere possible, including with the installation of a trunk lid made from sheet-molded compound. Taller buyers appreciated the extra inch of travel built into the driver's seat.

The best news of all was a power increase all around. The 3.8-liter V-6 jumped to 190 horsepower, and the 4.6-liter SOHC V-8—thanks to a higher-lift camshaft, coil-on-plug ignition, bigger valves, and a revised intake manifold—put out 260 horsepower.

Did You Know?
Ford commemorated the Mustang's 35th birthday with 5,000 limited edition coupes and convertibles that added $2,695 to the cost of a standard GT. These anniversary models came with a special raised hood scoop, a rear wing, distinctive side scoops, a black honeycomb deck lid appliqué, body-color rocker moldings, and a special aluminum shift knob.

The Cobra gained a long-awaited independent rear suspension (IRS) in 1999, which utilized short and long arms mounted on a tubular subframe. The system bolted directly to the same four mounting points found on the GT's solid rear axle, with the idea that other Mustang owners might want to perform an IRS upgrade. The IRS added 80 pounds of weight but reduced all-important *unsprung* weight by 125 pounds.

SVT engineers gave the 4.6-liter DOHC V-8 a different combustion chamber design and reconfigured intake port geometry to

1999 SVT COBRA

Price: $27,470 (Cobra coupe)
$31,470 (Cobra convertible)
Engine: 4.6-liter DOHC V-8, 320 horsepower
0–60 mph: 5.5 seconds
Top Speed: 160 mph
Production: 8,095

create a more efficient air/fuel mixture. The improved combustion boosted the powerplant to 320 horsepower. The new Cobra put its impressive power through a Borg-Warner-designed T-45 five-speed that had been greatly improved by moving its production to Tremec.

Unfortunately, SVT had a very embarrassing problem with the new Cobra. Car magazines reported that the Cobras they tested were actually slower than the previous model. Dynamometers revealed the new snake was not producing its advertised 320 horsepower, so SVT recalled all '99 Cobras already in private hands and prevented new ones from being sold until the problem could be addressed. SVT replaced the intake manifold, engine management computer, and exhaust system from the catalytic converter back on each car and then applied an "Authorized Modifications" label to the front of each engine compartment.

Did You Know?

In 1999, SVT nearly reached a perfect balance of sales when comparing Cobra coupes to convertibles. Of the 8,095 Cobras it built, 4,040 were closed cars and 4,055 were ragtops. Colors offered included Ultra White, Ebony, Rio Red, and Electric Green. Black was the most-popular color that year.

During its final three years, Saleen's S-351 was available only in supercharged form. In 1999, that package was rated at 495 horsepower, but it was at the end of its production because EPA provisions had run out. The model's biggest problem staying certified lay not in tailpipe emissions from the 5.8-liter pushrod V-8, but in evaporative emissions from the car's fuel system. Unlike Ford's current 4.6-liter engine, the 5.8 had never been converted to a returnless fuel delivery system. The S-351's setup allowed heat into the fuel lines on return from the

1999 SALEEN

Price: $27,990 (S-281 coupe)
$49,990 (S-351 coupe)
Engine: 4.6-liter SOHC V-8, 285 horsepower (S-281)
5.8-liter V-8, 495 horsepower (S-351)
0–60 mph: 4.7 seconds (S-351)
Top Speed: 170 mph (S-351)
Production: 373 (S-281)
46 (S-351)

engine; that created expansion, which led to evaporation into the atmosphere.

To meet standards for 1999, Saleen engineers designed a complicated method for cooling the gasoline with small fans that blew air through tubes into a special shroud that surrounded the tank.

On the less-expensive S-281's 4.6-liter V-8, Saleen added smaller-diameter accessory pulleys, a performance air filter, less-restrictive mufflers, freer-flowing exhaust pipes, and a computer programmed for premium unleaded. The result was a healthy 285 horsepower (up 25 from the standard GT on which it was based). Like the S-351, the S-281 was available in coupe or convertible form.

Two competition-ready SR models were built in 1999.

Did You Know?

Saleen built an in-house certification lab so it could develop power-enhancing systems for the Mustang's 4.6-liter SOHC V-8. The first product was its Series I Eaton supercharger option, which cost $3,995 and boosted the S-281's output to 350 horsepower. It went into production in April 1999 after passing its 50-state certification.

With a dark green Mustang fastback starring in the most-famous movie chase scene ever, it only made sense for Ford to release a commemorative edition. Steve McQueen's 1968 *Bullitt* made the Mustang a cinematic icon, as it flew through the hills of San Francisco in pursuit of a Dodge Charger.

In 2001, Ford offered a $3,695 Bullitt dress-up and performance package for its GT coupes that allowed us mortals a small sliver of McQueen mojo. That extra cash bought one of three model-unique colors—Dark Highland Green, True Blue, or Black—and a long list of mods that included special

2001 BULLITT

Price: $26,320
Engine: 4.6-liter V-8, 265 horsepower
0–60 mph: 5.8 seconds
Top Speed: 140 mph
Production: 5,582

side scoop caps, 17-inch American Racing aluminum wheels, a lowered suspension, modified C-pillars, quarter panel molding, a brushed aluminum fuel filler door, special Bullitt badging, and polished, rolled tailpipe tips. The interior was a successful retro design, recalling the late 1960s with chromed bezels, gauges with vintage fonts, and pleated seat vinyl.

The GT's standard 4.6-liter V-8 gained only five horsepower through a twin 57-millimeter throttle body, revised cast-aluminum intake manifold, and high-flow mufflers, but revalved struts and shocks, unique stabilizer bars in front and rear, frame rail connectors, and 13-inch Brembo front brakes made it feel like a different animal.

Did You Know?

Two 1968 Mustang fastbacks starred in the movie *Bullitt*. One was sent to the crusher, and the other was sold to an editor at the movie studio. In 1970, he sold the car to a police detective in New Jersey. In 1974, the surviving *Bullitt* Mustang went to its current owner, who prefers to remain anonymous.

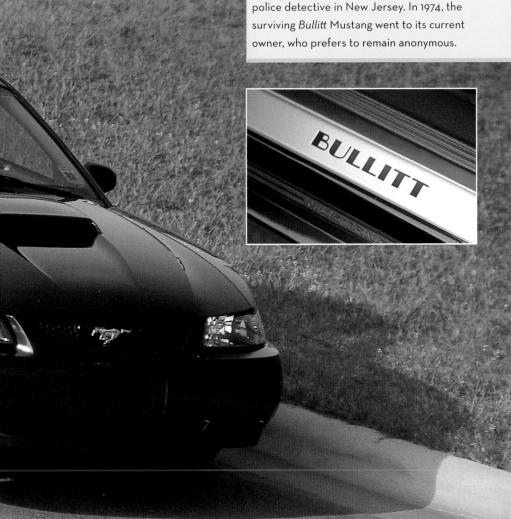

Jack Roush is well known to NASCAR fans because he has owned Cup cars driven by Mark Martin, Matt Kenseth, Jeff Burton, and Carl Edwards, but he also has been involved with every aspect of the automotive world, including research and development for the American automakers and performance engine building for a variety of applications.

Roush began producing performance packages for V-6 and V-8 Mustangs in 1997 that could be ordered through Ford

2001 ROUSH STAGE 3
Price: $48,975 (coupe)
Engine: 4.6-liter V-8, 360 horsepower
0–60 mph: 5.1 seconds
Top Speed: N/A
Production: 176

dealerships. For 2001, his Stage 1 package (available on V-6 or V-8 Mustangs) included a body kit, rear spoiler, and 17x8-inch argent wheels and tires. Stage 2 (only for GT

conversions) added 18-inch argent wheels and tires, plus a lowered performance suspension. At Stage 3 (GT only), buyers got an Eaton supercharger and computer recalibration that boosted output to 360 horsepower, an aluminum flywheel, subframe connectors, 17-inch wheels, a Cobra hood, and Roush's brake system.

A Stage 3 Rally model came with lowered suspension, 18-inch wheels, racing-style alloy pedals, and white-face gauges. All Stage 3

Roush Mustangs had plaques with individual serial numbers indicating year of production.

The seriously fast car in the Roush stable for 2001 was the 380R, which featured the supercharged engine, Cobra hood, cosmetic upgrades, plaque, and Roush brakes.

Did You Know?

Jack Roush's Stage 3 had the largest tires that could possibly fit the 2001 Mustang's wheel wells. They measured 265/35-18 in front and 295/35-18 in back. The Stage 3, the Saleen S-281, and the previous year's Cobra R were the only Mustangs with 18-inch wheels at the time.

During its short four years of life, the 1969 to 1973 first-generation Mach 1 was the most-popular performance package available. It made such a splash that in its introductory year alone Ford sold 72,000 fastback-only Mach 1 Mustangs. Like the GT that preceded it, the Mach 1 was powered by a V-8; depending on the model year, V-8 choices included everything from a base 302 to a 428 or 429 Super Cobra Jet.

The Mach 1's reputation suffered from 1974 to 1978, when the package was offered on the diminutive Mustang II 2+2 with a standard V-6 or the weak, extra-cost V-8. When Ford introduced the Mustang's third generation in 1979, the Mach 1 name disappeared from showrooms.

In 2003, Ford planners revived the model to fill a gap between the company's $24,305 GT coupe and $34,065 SVT Cobra. The

new Mach 1's $29,305 price tag fit squarely between the two, and its 305-horsepower DOHC V-8 (formerly the 1996 to 1998 Cobra engine) was a nice stopover on the way from the SOHC GT's 260 horses to the DOHC Cobra's 390 supercharged ponies. It also featured cosmetic upgrades reminiscent of the first-gen Mach 1 as well as four-wheel Brembo disc brakes. *Photos courtesy of Ford Motor Company.*

2003 MACH 1

Price: $29,305
Engine: 4.6-liter DOHC V-8, 305 horsepower
0–60 mph: 5.3 seconds
Top Speed: 160 mph
Production: 9,652

Did You Know?

The 2003 Mach 1 had a shaker intake scoop that visually dominated the hood and fed air to the ex-Cobra engine. Although the first-gen Mach 1's scoop shook from the violent output of the small- and big-block V-8s of the time, the modern Shaker rocked and rolled by way of springs and vacuum hoses.

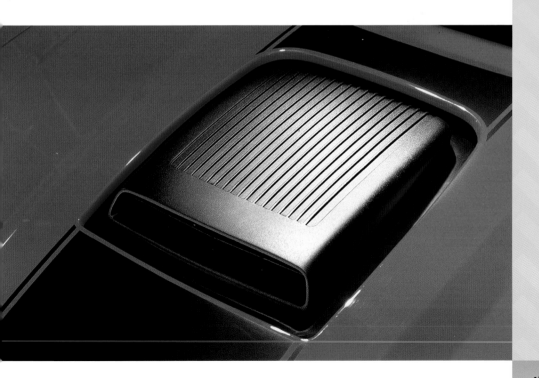

SVT's Cobra program produced no 2002 models but took a giant leap forward in 2003, easily surpassing performance benchmarks of the 1960s, such as the Boss 429 and Super Cobra Jet. The new Cobra carried an Eaton-supercharged 4.6-liter DOHC V-8 rated (conservatively, it would seem) at 390 horsepower and a six-speed manual transmission. The powerplant was based on a cast-iron block, breaking SVT's tradition of using aluminum blocks from 1996 to 2001, but it did share aluminum heads with that year's Mach 1.

2003 SVT COBRA

Price: $34,065 (coupe)
$38,405 (convertible)
Engine: 4.6-liter DOHC V-8, 390 horsepower
0–60 mph: 4.9 seconds
Top Speed: 155 mph
Production: 2,003 (10th Anniversary Edition)
13,476 (all 2003 production)

The supercharger was a Roots-type blower set up to produce eight pounds of boost, and a water-to-air intercooler reduced the

temperature of the charge for maximum mixture volatility.

The 2003 Cobra featured a heavy-duty clutch, strengthened U-joints and half shafts, and a new aluminum driveshaft. The rear axle ratio was dropped from 3.27:1 to 3.55:1 in the interest of quicker acceleration. The '03 Cobra used a refined version of the independent rear suspension SVT introduced on the '99 model.

To understand just how far the Cobra name had progressed since the dark performance days of the 1970s, note that the 2003 put out more than three times the horsepower of the 1976 to 1978 Cobra II and '78 King Cobra V-8s.

Did You Know?

SVT celebrated the 10th birthday of its Mustang-based Cobra in 2003 with special coupes and convertibles that featured 17x9-inch argent wheels, red leather seating surfaces, carbon fiber–like interior trim, and unique anniversary badging on the floor mats and deck lid. Exterior colors included Black, Torch Red, and Silver Metallic.

In 1964, during the launch of the phenomenally successful Mustang, Jack Roush was a 22-year-old engineer working for Ford Motor Company. He formed Jack Roush Performance Engineering after leaving in 1976 and started Roush Racing in 1988. Roush was a professional drag racer who enjoyed success in NASCAR, SCCA, Trans-Am, IMSA, and IRL. Today, his engine-building company supplies

2003 ROUSH BOYD CODDINGTON CALIFORNIA ROADSTER

Price: $42,000
$48,000 (supercharged)
Engine: 4.6-liter SOHC V-8, 260 horsepower
4.6-liter SOHC supercharged V-8, 360 horsepower
0–60 mph: N/A
Top Speed: N/A
Production: 100

racing engines for several NASCAR teams, and his Roush Industries provides engineering and development support for the Big Three automakers.

In 2003, Roush collaborated with hot rod legend Boyd Coddington to create a limited run of 100 convertibles built around Roush Performance Products' Stage 2 and Stage 3 Mustang equipment, specifically aerodynamic body pieces,

sport leather seats, a convertible light bar, serial-numbered plaques, and 18-inch wheels and tires. The drop tops, known as the Boyd Coddington California Roadsters, were available in red, yellow, or silver, with black hoods.

Coddington designed the 18-inch Smoothie II chromed wheels—18x9 in front, 18x10 in back—and autographed the white-face gauges. Roush's Stage 3 suspension changes included shorter springs (1.5 inches lower in front, 1.0 inch in the rear), Bilstein monotube shocks and struts, and a new 35-millimeter front sway bar.

Did You Know?

Of the 100 Roush Boyd Coddington California Roadsters, 75 were naturally aspirated and 25 had the supercharged, 360-horsepower SOHC engines. When Steve Chirrik, a former Roush employee, and Boyd Coddington Jr. conceived the roadster program, they intended it to be a West Coast promotion only.

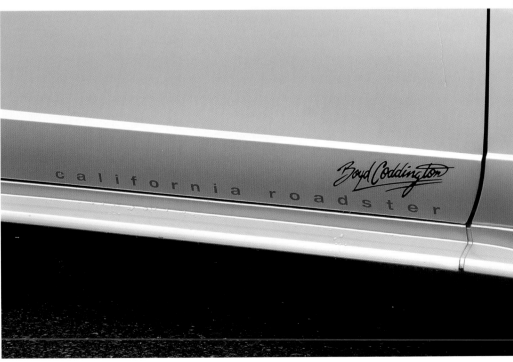

CHAPTER 5
FIFTH GENERATION: RETRO MANIA

Although conceptual prototypes had been seen in magazines all over the world, the production version of the 2005 Mustang was introduced at the 2004 North American International Auto Show in Detroit. It was based on Ford's D2C (D-class, two-door coupe) platform, which was itself an offshoot of the corporate DEW98 rear-drive chassis found under the Lincoln LS, Ford Thunderbird, and Jaguar S-Type. The engineering code name for the '05 Mustang development was S-197.

Its new design represented a smooth blend of elements from the 1966 Shelby GT-350, '69 Mach 1, and early GTs. Even the legendary spinner hubcap showed itself on the base model wheels. Ford retained the Mustang's traditional long hood and short trunk proportions. The car's sides featured C-shaped indentions similar to what was found on the 1965 to 1966 models, and the new Mustang's three-element vertical taillamps mimic those on the early cars. Credit for the retro styling goes to chief engineer Hau Thai-Tang and designer Sid Ramnarace.

The S-197 was larger in every way than the 1994 to 2004 SN-95. It was longer (187.6 versus 183.2 inches), wider (73.9 versus 73.1), taller (54.5 versus 53.1), and had a longer wheelbase (107.1 versus 101.3). Even fuel capacity increased, rising from 15.7 to 16 gallons. Surprisingly, there was very little weight gain with the 2005; the V-6 model was 10 pounds heavier (to 3,300 pounds), and the GT put on 103 pounds (to 3,450).

Powerplants saw substantial improvements. The V-6, now displacing 4.0 liters and wearing single overhead camshafts, produced 210 horsepower with a 6,100-rpm redline. (This rating was a milestone of sorts because it meant the base engine put out more horsepower than the 1972 to 1986 5.0-liter V-8s.) Base cars received a Tremec T-5 five-speed manual transmission but could be upgraded to a five-speed automatic. Mustangs ordered with the GT package received a 300-horsepower 4.6-liter SOHC V-8 that was manually shifted by a Tremec 3650 five-speed or extra-cost 5R55S automatic. Mustangs with V-8s and manual transmissions were fitted with 3.55:1 rear axle gears; all others received 3.31:1 ratios.

It may have been named for a World War II warbird, but the Mustang went jet-fighter high-tech in 2005. Ford saved 75 pounds by switching the V-8 engine's block from cast iron to aluminum. Three-valve heads (two intake, one exhaust) with variable valve timing created a V-8 that could rev all the way to 6,250. Although it had served

the Mustang well for 40 years, Ford threw out mechanical linkage between the gas pedal and the engine's intake; instead, the new pony's throttle was entirely controlled electronically, as was the five-speed automatic transmission. A "limp home" mode was built into the computer's program that allows the engine to alternate firing on half its cylinders if a cooling system leak or sensor failure is detected. Although it added more weight, a two-piece driveshaft was used in the GT to ensure smooth delivery of its 300 horsepower.

Even the 2005 Mustang's assembly plant was different. The Mustang's home from 1964 to 2004 had been Dearborn Assembly, although additional plants were used in the early years to meet the high demand. More than 6.7 million Mustangs came from the Dearborn location, but Ford decided its state-of-the-art Auto Alliance International factory in Flat Rock should build this next generation. The AAI was created by Ford and Mazda as a joint venture to produce their Probe and MX-6 two-door sporty cars in the late 1980s. Relocation of the Mustang to AAI marked the first time front-drive Mazda models were assembled on the same line as a rear-drive product.

After a successful public reception and many strong-selling nostalgia models, such as the Bullitt, GT/CS, and Shelby GT-500KR, the S-197 was restyled for 2010. Every body panel except the coupe's roof was replaced, resulting in a leaner look that lowered drag coefficient by 4 percent on base models and 7 percent on the GTs. While the 2010 V-6 engine was unchanged, Ford made the 2008 to 2009 Bullitt's 315-horsepower V-8 standard in the GT. *Photo courtesy of Ford Motor Company.*

FIFTH GENERATION: RETRO MANIA

Keeping things simple, Ford offered four new Mustang models when the 2005 season began—a Deluxe and Premium V-6 coupe and a Deluxe and Premium GT coupe. The convertible, which appeared in showrooms later in the spring, followed the same pattern.

The base Mustang came nicely equipped with the 4.0-liter SOHC V-6, Tremec T-5

2005

Price: $19,410 (V-6 coupe)
$24,995 (GT coupe)
Engine: 4.0-liter SOHC V-6, 210 horsepower
4.6-liter SOHC V-8, 300 horsepower
0–60 mph: 5.2 seconds (GT coupe)
Top Speed: 150 mph (GT coupe)

five-speed manual transmission, four-wheel power disc brakes, painted 16x7-inch aluminum wheels, and all power equipment. Moving up to the Premium trim level added bright 16-inch aluminum wheels with chromed spinners, the Shaker 500 audio system with six-disc CD changer and MP3 capability, power driver's seat, and leather. A GT Deluxe brought the 4.6-liter V-8 engine, ABS, stainless dual exhaust, fog lamps, reflector halogen headlights, rear spoiler, 17-inch painted aluminum wheels, and other creature comforts. Choosing the GT Premium added the Shaker 500 and leather-trimmed sport bucket seats.

For Mustang enthusiasts who really had to have it all, the Interior Upgrade Package, which was available on all models, brought the bright instrument cluster with adjustable colors, leather shift knob, and other niceties. The Interior Color Accent Package, which required the Interior Upgrade Package, had red leather seating surfaces, inserts, and floor mats. *Photos courtesy of Ford Motor Company.*

Did You Know?

The 2005 Mustang brought many firsts to the line, including the first aluminum-block V-8 in a non-Cobra Mustang, the first single overhead camshaft V-6 engine, the first five-speed automatic transmission, and the first three-valve heads.

The fifth-generation Mustang's strong V-8 and 1960s-era styling immediately inspired many over-the-top variations, including the awesome Shadrach from Pure Power Motorsports.

From a small shop in Marietta, Georgia, Mike Langston and crew converted a limited number of new Mustang GTs into $175,000 super-ponies, starting with the tall, chrome-covered engines. Stock 4.6-liter V-8s were stripped to the block and then rebuilt with ported, three-valve heads; a 16-injector fuel system that allowed docile highway driving but opened up like a four-barrel Holley

2005 PLATT & PAYNE SIGNATURE EDITION SHADRACH MUSTANG

Price: $175,000
Engine: 4.6-liter turbocharged SOHC V-8, 900 horsepower
0–60 mph: N/A
Top Speed: 175 mph (est.)

for all-out performance; twin water-to-air Precision T3 turbochargers with dual-stage boost control; dual water-to-air intercoolers; and a Kinsler 8-Stack injection system.

The result was an astounding 900 horsepower handled by a G-Force six-speed racing transmission and a Strange Ford nine-inch rear with 3.55:1 gears.

The chassis was just as impressive, with a new AJE K-member up front, a competition-grade suspension throughout, and Brembo cross-drilled rotors not at all hidden by four 20-inch Weld Racing wheels and Nitto tires.

Leather-wrapped Recaro front seats with integral air-conditioning and heat, a six-point chromoly roll cage, and G-Force five-point harnesses made the interior a serious place to be. Outside, Shadrach's all-business aerodynamic aids were designed to keep the Sonic Blue coupe planted up to an estimated top speed in excess of 175 miles per hour.

Did You Know?

The Platt & Payne Signature Edition of the Shadrach Mustang commemorated 1960s Ford drag racers Hubert Platt and Randy Payne—two Georgians whose blue race cars were known collectively as "The Going Thing." Platt's cars were named Georgia Shaker or some variation; Payne's nickname was Mr. Big Stuff.

Here is another great idea from the 1960s that only got better when revived 40 years later.

In 1966, Carroll Shelby sold 1,001 of his Mustang-based GT-350 fastbacks to the Hertz rental car agency for use in its Sports Car Club. This very unusual fleet sale accounted for nearly 40 percent of that year's Shelby production. Many of the Hertz cars were painted black with gold stripes and fitted with manual transmissions, but records show they were made in other colors and that most cars were shipped with automatic transmissions. The 306-horsepower 289-cubic-inch V-8 probably made many travelers consider buying either a Shelby or standard Mustang.

In 2006, Shelby sold a batch of 500 identical black-and-gold GT-350H fastbacks to Hertz (for its Fun Collection) with 4.6-liter SOHC V-8s putting 325 horsepower through five-speed automatic transmissions and 3.55:1 axle gears. Every aspect of the '66 rental car was reproduced in some way

2006 - 2007 SHELBY HERTZ

Price: rental only
Engine: 4.6-liter SOHC V-8, 325 horsepower
0–60 mph: N/A
Top Speed: N/A
Production: 500 (2006)
500 (2007)

CSM No. 07H296

n the '06, including the wide gold stripes, ocker panel callouts, hood pins, grille reatment, and interior decor.

In spite of pleas to purchase them irectly from the factory, all 500 cars were ut into rental duty and then run through osed auctions.

For 2007, Hertz bought 500 more copies of the same car, but in convertible form.

In case you weren't around in 1970, Parnelli Jones ruled the Sports Car Club of America's Trans-Am Series in a Grabber Orange Boss 302 Mustang. Over the course of his career, the versatile driver also competed successfully in NASCAR, off-road, Indy, Formula One, and Midget racing.

In 1987, he helped Saleen Autosport clinch its first SCCA championship. To commemorate the 20th anniversary of that win, Saleen Inc. produced a limited run of

2007 SALEEN/PARNELLI JONES

Price: $59,015
Engine: 5.0-liter SOHC V-8, 400 horsepower
0–60 mph: N/A
Top Speed: N/A
Production: 500

500 identical Parnelli Jones replicas that did a good imitation of his original Boss 302 race car. Starting with the stock Mustang GT engine, Saleen built a 302-cubic-inch,

three-valve, SOHC V-8 specifically for this model that produced 400 horsepower. It was backed by a quick-ratio five-speed manual transmission and 3.73:1 rear axle gears.

Additional retro touches included period-correct Grabber paint, Shaker hood scoop, 302 striping, rear louvers, black rear wing, side scoops, and competition-style hood pins. Even Jones' No. 15 decal was reproduced as a removable vinyl graphic. The 19-inch wheels were faithful

interpretations of the Minilites fitted to PJ's original Trans-Am ride, and they hid 14-inch slotted rotors in front, 11.8-inch discs in back.

Did You Know?

In 1962, Parnelli Jones was the first driver to qualify for the Indianapolis 500 at a speed faster than 150 miles per hour. He qualified on the pole in 1962 and 1963, and he won the 1963 running of the traditional Memorial Day race.

Hollywood loves a remake, but while no one has yet dared throw together a modern version of Steve McQueen's 1968 *Bullitt*, which starred a 390 GT 2+2, Ford produced its second model inspired by that movie in 2008.

Just like the 1968 original and 2001 sequel, the '08 Bullitt is a Highland Green fastback devoid of ornamental chrome, galloping ponies, and foglights. With its grayed-out, five-spoke, 18-inch retro rims and dark-cave interior, it is the perfect car for blending into traffic while tailing a suspect—as long as the perp is not a *Bullitt* fan.

The Bullitt features a slightly warmed-up version of the standard GT's 4.6-liter SOHC three-valve engine. Changes to cold-air induction, computer programming, and

a louder exhaust bump Bullitt's output to 315 horsepower and push the redline up 250 revs to 6,500 rpm. The Mustang GT's five-speed manual is the only available transmission, and it feeds power back to 3.73:1 gears in the rear. Suspension upgrades won't let you get airborne in San Francisco, but they do contribute to a grippy 0.84g of lateral acceleration.

2008 BULLITT
Price: $31,525
Engine: 4.6-liter SOHC V-8, 315 horsepower
0–60 mph: 5.0 seconds
Top Speed: 151 mph
Production: 7,700

The front seats and steering wheel were taken from SVT's Shelby GT-500, and a wide panel of engine-turned aluminum across the dashboard complements the 1960s retro interior. *Photos by Al Rogers*

Did You Know?
Ford only produced 7,700 Bullitt models in 2008—most in Highland Green, although Black was offered. Due to demand, the company turned out another 3,300 for 2009, with no changes to the Bullitt package. In all respects, the '08 Bullitt is faster than a stock '68 390 GT.

Steve Saleen was in the habit of producing a limited-edition anniversary model every five years, but he left his self-named company in 2007, just before its 25th birthday. To celebrate a quarter-century in the high-performance Mustang business—and to give a preview of the resources his new enterprise had—he built a single Twenty-Fifth Anniversary Mustang Concept.

The first Mustang to fly the SMS Ltd. banner, this special pony is motivated by a supercharged SOHC, three-valve V-8

2008 SMS TWENTY-FIFTH ANNIVERSARY

Price: $100,000 (est.)
Engine: 4.6-liter SOHC supercharged V-8, 720 horsepower
0–60 mph: N/A
Top Speed: N/A
Production: 1

stroked to 5.0 liters of displacement. Output is 720 horsepower, which is fed through a six-speed manual transmission. Not one to

underestimate the value of an eye-catching design, Steve Mark Saleen (the three names whose initials make up the company's name) created hood-mounted Red Butterfly air flaps that pop open under full throttle and a Light Blade LED taillight treatment with sequential turn signals. Carbon-fiber side splitters and rear diffuser recall the front and rear of Saleen's S7 supercar.

This one-off anniversary special wears Chromosome Silver, a BASF paint that reflects light like no previous treatment.

Its interior sports Saleen's traditional yellow, black, and white racing colors, which show off nicely under the car's tinted glass roof.

Did You Know?

Steve Saleen's first anniversary car, 1988's SA-5, was also a one-off product. It was built to develop the engine and chassis for the 1989-only SSC. With the SA-5 and this latest model, there have been a total of 27 anniversary Saleen Mustangs, including nine 1993 SA-10s, ten 2008 SA-15s, and six 2003 SA-20s.

In the twenty-first century, the best way to design a new car is to look at an old one.

For example, the 1968 Shelby GT-500KR— a mid-year introduction sporting a 428-cubic-inch Cobra Jet V-8—has become one of the most valuable cars in the Mustang hobby, so when Carroll Shelby began applying his name to Ford's modern high-performance ponies, no one was surprised to hear that a world-dominating KR was in the works. Taking advantage of the original

2008 SHELBY GT-500KR

Price: $79,995
Engine: 5.4-liter DOHC supercharged V-8, 540 horsepower
0–60 mph: 4.0 seconds
Top Speed: 195 mph
Production: 1,571 (inc. 2008–09 production for domestic market)

model's 40-year anniversary, his company introduced its new GT-500KR in mid-2008.

This modern "King of the Road" looked very much like the original, but it had an engine that would blow away anything from the late 1960s—a supercharged 5.4-liter DOHC V-8 that produced 540 horsepower! With a six-speed manual transmission and dragstrip-friendly 3.73:1 rear axle ratio, the KR could run to 60 from a stop in four seconds. Quarter-mile times were in the 11.9 range at 120 miles per hour on stock rubber.

The KR was also the most-expensive production Mustang ever, with a sticker just south of $80K. Shelby planned to build exactly 1,571 units (over a two-year period) in order to match the original car's numbers.

Did You Know?

The '08 KR was not only expensive to buy—it cost a lot to repair, as well. One owner was shocked to discover that a replacement for his damaged carbon-fiber hood would cost $18,400. When this information was made public, Shelby lowered the price to $9,700.

Legendary engine builder Jack Roush combined his love of aviation with an ability to get maximum performance from a Ford V-8 and created the P-51A Mustang—a 510-horsepower pavement-eater named for America's most-powerful World War II–era fighter plane.

The Roush crew in Livonia, Michigan, began with a standard Mustang GT and improved its 4.6-liter V-8 by stripping it to the block and installing a new intake manifold, forged aluminum pistons, unique 52-pound-an-hour injectors, fuel rails, dual 60-millimeter

2008 ROUSH P-51A

Price: $32,103 plus '08 Mustang GT
Engine: 4.6-liter SOHC supercharged V-8, 510 horsepower
0–60 mph: N/A
Top Speed: N/A
Production: 151

electronic throttle bodies, a cold-air induction system, and a ROUSHcharger supercharger. The result of these upgrades was an output of 510 horsepower.

The aircraft-inspired supercar also received Roush's Stage 3 suspension components, competition-grade four-wheel disc brake rotors, and 18-inch chromed alloy wheels. Aerodynamic Roush body panels were fitted to the exterior, and the passenger compartment received leather sports seating and other equipment specific to the P-51A model.

During the car's debut at the Specialty Equipment Market Association trade show in Las Vegas in 2007, Jack Roush announced he would only build 100 examples, but, a few months later, dealer response persuaded him to increase production to 151.

Did You Know?

The P-51A's silver-and-black body mimics the fuselage of a typical World War II fighter plane. All Roush P-51As wear red-and-yellow checkered fender badges that commemorate the 357th Fighter Group—Mustang pilots whose 695 air victories over England and Germany ranked the highest in the Eighth Air Force.

2008 ROUSH P-51A

The year 2010 brought significant changes to the Mustang's body (every panel except the roof was new), interior, suspension, and power, but it retained the S-197 platform introduced in 2005. It is, therefore, a continuation of the fifth generation.

Designers abandoned the blocky shape of the 2005 to 2009 models, pinching off the front and rear and making the grille lean more readily into the wind. Small wheels became a thing of the past as Ford offered only a range of rims measuring 17 to 19 inches in diameter. Components introduced on the 2008 Bullitt model moved to the GT, such as the tower-to-tower chassis brace, polished-aluminum shift knob, and 3.5-inch exhaust tips.

2010

Price: $20,995 (V-6 coupe)
$27,995 (GT coupe)
Engine: 4.0-liter SOHC V-6, 210 horsepower
4.6-liter SOHC V-8, 315 horsepower
0–60 mph: 5.0 seconds (GT coupe)
Top Speed: 151 mph (GT coupe)

The base 4.0-liter SOHC V-6 retained its 210 horsepower, but the GT moved up to the former Bullitt powerplant—a 315-horsepower three-valve V-8 calibrated to run on regular fuel as well as premium.

Improvements abounded throughout the redesigned S-197, including relocating the radio antenna to the rear fender (finally!), an innovative EasyFuel capless gas-fill system, standard AdvanceTrack electronic stability control, and a sound induction tube on GT models that pipes V-8 music into the passenger compartment. Three-element LED taillamps fire sequentially from the inboard element out, recalling the '65 Thunderbird and '68 Shelby. *Photos courtesy of Ford Motor Company.*

Did You Know?

In a three-car comparison test against the Dodge Challenger R/T and Chevrolet Camaro SS, *Car and Driver* gave the 2010 Mustang GT the highest marks. This surprised the magazine's staff, as the Ford had the least horsepower of the trio and only had a five-speed transmission; the Chevy and Dodge had six-speeds.

With its 5.4-liter V-8, the latest Shelby GT-500 is officially the most-powerful factory Mustang in history. Using lessons learned from the 2008 GT-500KR (as well as hundreds of aftermarket tuners), Ford engineers massaged 540 horsepower from the supercharged and intercooled DOHC powerplant.

Overdrive gears in the Shelby's six-speed manual transmission were reconfigured for lower revs at highway speed, while the rear axle's gear ratio was bumped from 3.31:1 to 3.55:1 for stronger acceleration. (The gearing changes netted an EPA highway rating of 22 miles per gallon—

2010 SHELBY GT-500

Price: $46,325 (coupe)
$51,325 (convertible)
Engine: 5.4-liter DOHC V-8, 540 horsepower
0–60 mph: 4.5 seconds
Top Speed: 161 mph

an improvement over 2009's 20 miles per gallon.)

The coupe wears 19-inch forged aluminum wheels with Goodyear F1 Supercar tires, while the convertible has 18s all around. Body enhancements include an aggressive hood scoop intended to remove heat from the engine compartment and a "Gurney Flap" spoiler for adjusting rear downforce.

The interior benefits from upgrades, such as all-leather seating, real aluminum on the instrument panel, and a redesigned short-throw shifter. The SVT team created a white shift knob that is visually split by twin racing stripes.

The '10 Shelby is also one of the heaviest factory Mustangs ever, weighing in at 3,897 pounds—about 300 pounds more than the standard Mustang GT. *Photos courtesy of Shelby American Inc.*

Did You Know?

Ford's Noise, Vibration, and Harshness (NVH) team used some interesting technology to tune the V-8's intake sound. They placed a resonator between the air filter and engine throttle body that automatically reacts to muffle unwanted noises without restricting airflow.

In 2007, Jack Roush added the 427R to his lineup of Stage 1, 2, and 3 Mustangs. For $43,375, the supercharged 427R had a smidge more horsepower than the Stage 3 (427 vs. 415) due to computer calibration and a different exhaust system, making it the most-powerful Mustang ever produced by Roush Performance. This top-performance model included Roush's unique body kit, 18-inch chrome wheels, a competition-grade suspension, and special striping and badging, but left off some of the Stage 3's less-necessary equipment. Buyers wanting to spend more money opted for 14-inch front brakes, a short-throw shifter, leather sport seats, white-faced gauges, and carbon-fiber dash trim.

For 2010, the $43,071 Model 427R put out 435 horsepower and featured a new ROUSHcharger supercharger/intercooler setup. The 427R's less-is-more philosophy was retained, and the model included only the hot V-8, appearance package, 18-inch chromed wheels, Roush suspension package, and call-out stripes. Everything else was standard Mustang GT, unless ordered otherwise. Options included white-face gauges, an upgraded exhaust, sport leather

seating, a light bar (convertibles only), bigger brakes, and Roush's clever tool kit that mounts under the trunk lid. *Photos courtesy of ROUSH Performance Products Inc.*

2010 ROUSH 427R

Price: $43,071
Engine: 4.6-liter supercharged SOHC V-8, 435 horsepower
0–60 mph: 4.7 seconds
Top Speed: N/A

Did You Know?

The original 427R got its name from the fact that it put out 427 horsepower and because Ford enthusiasts have a soft spot for those three digits, having fallen in love with its 427-cubic-inch drag-racing V-8 during the late 1960s. The 427-cubic-inch V-8 was never officially installed in a production Mustang.

INDEX